how to build
OUTDOOR
FURNITURE

Donald R. Brann

THIRD PRINTING — 1983

Published by
EASI-BILD DIRECTIONS SIMPLIFIED, INC.
Briarcliff Manor, NY 10510

Library of Congress Card No. 76–14045

684.18

FIRST PRINTING
© 1976

REVISED EDITIONS
1978, 1983

ISBN 0-87733-754-3

NOTE   4-84   Publ 795
Due to the variance in quality and availability of many materials and
products, always follow directions a manufacturer and/or retailer offers.
Unless products are used exactly as the manufacturer specifies, its war-
ranty can be voided. While the author mentions certain products by trade
name, no endorsement or end use guarantee is implied. In every case the
author suggests end uses as specified by the manufacturer prior to
publication.

Since manufacturers frequently change ingredients or formula and/or
introduce new and improved products, or fail to distribute in certain
areas, trade names are mentioned to help the reader zero in on products
of comparable quality and end use.   The Publisher

LEARN TO RELAX

As every medical report confirms, learning to relax is an important part of staying healthy and alive. While millions now have more leisure time than any previous generation, relatively few use or enjoy this God-given gift in a truly constructive way.

To fully appreciate how much extra living you can still get out of each spare hour, and to release your mind from the pressure of TV violence, read through this book. Note each illustration. After completing the first reading, ask yourself two questions: Was every step clear? Did the author use any words or steps of construction difficult to grasp? Everyone who can read should be able to follow every step. This creates confidence. Building one chair provides a change of pace — building several, complete escape.

The exceptionally simple and honest design of each project appeals to all ages, youngsters in manual training to retirees with too much time. To insure complete success, full size patterns simplify tracing all curved parts.

Getting the workbench habit is one way to materially reduce tension. Building the outdoor furniture described in this book provides a fun way to escape. Learning to reshape the lifestyle of the person you see in the mirror each morning doesn't require any special therapy. It does require a willingness to do today what you didn't think you could do yesterday. TRY — discover The Real You.

Don R. Brann

TABLE OF CONTENTS

OUTDOOR LIVING

Creating a comfortable place to unwind encourages relaxation. Placing these sturdy, handsome pieces where they can be used when desired is comparable to seeing a roadsign before reaching a fork in a road. The Briarcliff lawn chair, Illus. 1, is one of the most popular outdoor chairs ever built. It first appeared in an Easi-Bild full size pattern many years ago. Thousands were built each year for personal use, additional thousands for resale.

A matching settee, Illus. 2, a child size chair, Illus. 3, plus a table, Illus. 4, make a handsome set. When painted white, blue or even pink, they sell quickly. Other popular pieces of easy to build furniture are the chaise lounge, Illus. 5, a picnic table, Illus. 6, and a modernized version of the old fashioned lawn glider, Illus. 7.

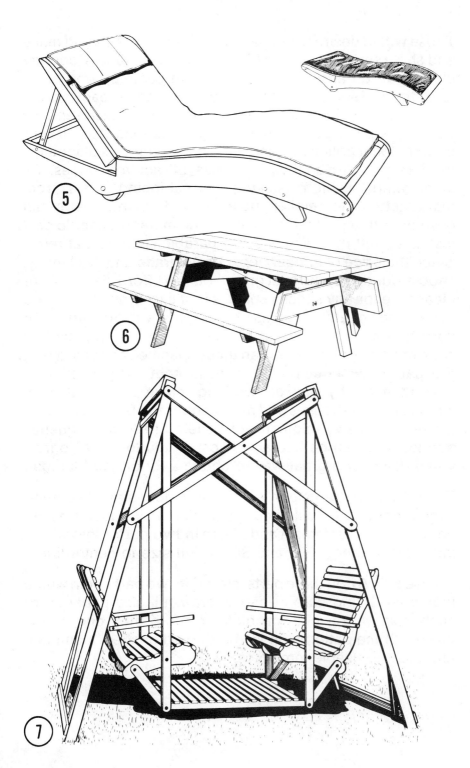

5

6

7

9

Those with a desire to start a part time business should make and show samples of each piece to motel managers, country clubs, garden and home improvement centers, even furniture stores. If someone with the same idea has already beaten a path to their door, sell direct to the public. Place samples where people can see them, in gas stations, etc. If your church, local police auxiliary or favorite charity is planning a fund raising drive, these projects attract top prices. By eliminating skyhigh packing and shipping costs from manufacturer to retailer, building and selling chairs can develop into a profitable business. All materials should cost less than half the price of a comparable chair sold at retail. Since the price of lumber depends on grade and availability, shop around. Buy the best grade you can afford. If you ask for clear pine, or any special species that's in short supply, you have to pay dearly. If you ask for #2 pine with tight knots, or have a chance to pick out boards, you can frequently find shorter or longer lengths than those specified and still lay out the pattern without hitting a loose knot. If you plan on making a hobby of woodworking, make inquiry at local wholesale warehouses and manufacturing plants, especially those that receive shipments on pallets. These are frequently surplus and can be had at no cost. If you locate a source, you'll discover a great way to obtain a lot of good lumber.

The full size patterns printed on the foldout simplify cutting curved parts. Due to limited space, part JA is superimposed on A; JG on G. Patterns A and SF are in two parts. Join where indicated. Patterns F, E and SE are full size to center line.

Chaise side A is in three parts, cleat C in two parts. Join where indicated. Using carbon paper, draw full size patterns for each part. If you plan on building more than one of any project, trace patterns on ⅛" hardboard or sheet aluminum and make reusable templates.

TOOLS

From the earliest times, craftsmen built houses and the finest pieces of furniture, cabinetry, etc., using hand tools. While many of the tools were crude compared to today's standard, museum quality craftsmanship was commonplace. A coping saw, square, brace and assorted bits, cross cut and rip saw are about the most important tools needed. Having access to a saber saw, electric drill and sander can save considerable time and labor. Those beginning to assemble tools should buy the finest quality they can afford. Good tools provide a sound, lifetime investment. Consider money invested in tools as you would premiums on health insurance. Both generate peace of mind.

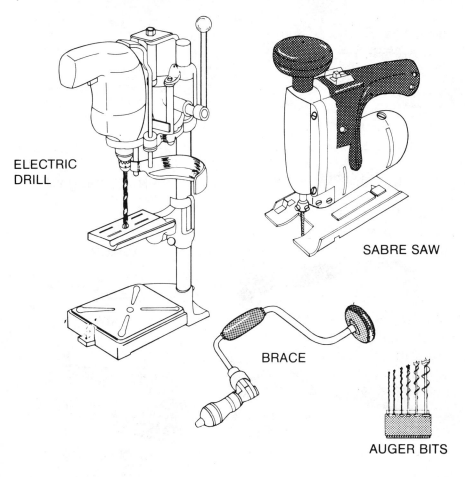

ELECTRIC
DRILL

SABRE SAW

BRACE

AUGER BITS

11

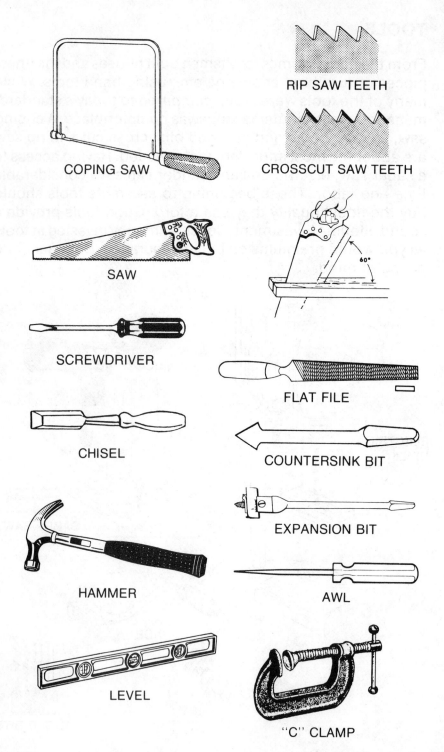

COPING SAW

RIP SAW TEETH

CROSSCUT SAW TEETH

SAW

60°

SCREWDRIVER

FLAT FILE

CHISEL

COUNTERSINK BIT

EXPANSION BIT

HAMMER

AWL

LEVEL

"C" CLAMP

HELPFUL HINTS

The solid outside line and shaded area on the full size pattern printed on the foldout indicate overall shape. The dash lines show relative position of part indicated. Since thickness of lumber and/or saw cut can alter overall size, only drill holes when directions specify same. Placing parts in position permits drilling hole in adjoining part exactly where it's required.

All full size parts for the Briarcliff Chair are designated A,B,C,D,E,F,G,H,J,K. Parts for the settee are designated A,SB,SC,D,SE,SF,G,SH,J,K,SL. Parts for the Junior Briarcliff Chair are designated JA,JB,JC,JD,JE,JF,JG,JH,JJ,JK.

Always start with part A and work your way through B,C,D, etc. Follow step by step directions and you will not only have fun building each piece, but also feel feet taller everytime it's used.

Always check the end of each board with a square, Illus. 8, before measuring length. Use a sharp pencil to draw an accurate line.

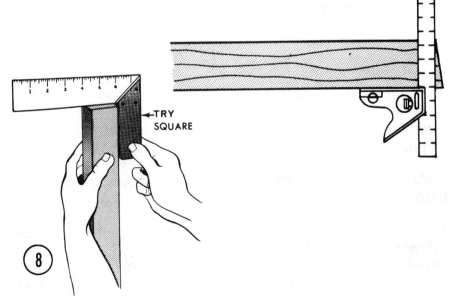

←TRY SQUARE

8

To simplify building and to insure top quality results, alternate methods of fastening are shown. Use a lag screw, hanger bolt, or cap screw and Teenut, Illus. 8A.

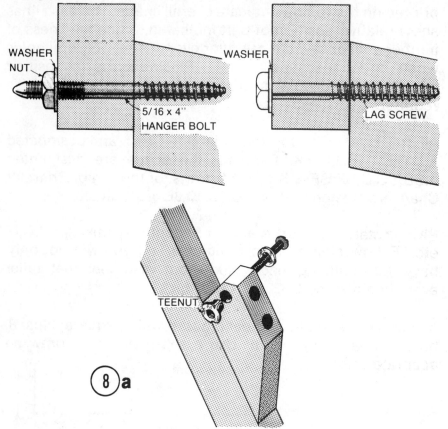

WASHER
NUT

5/16 x 4"
HANGER BOLT

WASHER

LAG SCREW

TEENUT

8 a

+ indicates approximate position of a screw hole. Check location of all parts before applying glue. Use waterproof glue on all outdoor furniture. Drill screw holes, apply glue to area of contact. Dip screw in glue before fastening parts together.

Prime coat the assembled piece with wood preservative before applying exterior paint.

Because some folks are small and thin while others may be tall and heavy, a large chair can be as uncomfortable to a small person as a small chair is to those with a large frame. When arms G are cut to full width of pattern G, Illus. 9, and

14

fastened in position to JH as indicated by dash lines on pattern G, it provides approximately 15½" clearance between the arms at the narrowest point. Trim inside edge to shape shown, Illus. 10, and it provides an opening measuring 17". Arm G will still project ½" over inside face of J. Cut arm G flush with J and you pick up another 1" clearance.

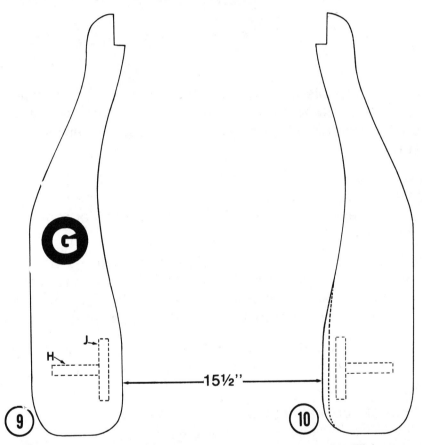

Seat slat B, front rail C, seat cleat E measure 19". This permits building a truly comfortable chair for the average size person. If those over six feet and others who weigh more than 200 lbs. find the space between arms a bit tight, instead of cutting B, C and E 19" as directions specify, cut each 21". Only add additional length to the straight parts at the ends of E. Keep curved part in exact position shown on pattern. Add extra length to ends of F. Only drill holes through F after placing it in position over end of K.

Countersink all screws. Bore a shank and pilot hole to size indicated, Illus. 11. This permits driving screws accurately and lessens chance of splitting wood. Bore 3/16" shank hole for a #10 screw. Bore a 3/32" pilot hole for a #10 screw.

COUNTERSINK

SHANK HOLE

PILOT HOLE

Always bore hole slightly less than diameter of threaded portion of screw and only half the depth of threaded area. Use a countersink bit to bevel edge of hole so it receives head of screw.

Lay out full size patterns on lumber specified. While a 1 x 6 formerly measured ¾ x 5⅝", then ¾ x 5½", same may now be slightly less. A 5½", even 5⅜" width is still OK for chair and settee side A and leg J.

Due to the variance in lumber width and thickness and the difference frequently created by sawcuts, always check size of additional parts after you begin assembly. You can then cut each to size required rather than size specified.

If directions specify drilling a hole in one part, place it in position required, mark and drill a matching hole.

At time of publication, stock lumber measured:

1 x 3 —	¾ x 2½"
1 x 6 —	¾ x 5½"
1 x 8 —	¾ x 7¼"
1 x 10 —	¾ x 9¼"
2 x 3 —	1½ x 2½"
2 x 4 —	1½ x 3½"
2 x 6 —	1½ x 5½"
2 x 10 —	1½ x 9¼"
2 x 12 —	1½ x 11¼"
5/4 x 12 —	1 1/16 x 11 to 11¼"

BRIARCLIFF LAWN CHAIR

One chair with 19'' seat slats requires the following material:

LIST OF MATERIALS
    1 — 1 x 6 x 10' - A,J
    1 — 1 x 2 x 8' - B
    1 — 1 x 2 x 10' - B
    2 — 1 x 4 x 12' - C,D,E
    1 — 1 x 8 x 8' - F,G,H,K
    8 — ¼ x 2'' cap screws or stove bolts
    8 — ¼'' Teenuts
  44 — 1½'' # 10 flathead wood screws

Illus. 12 shows how to lay out parts A and J on a 1 x 6 x 10'. Illus. 13 shows F, G, K and H on a 1 x 8 x 8'. Illus. 14 shows parts B on a 1 x 2 x 8' and a 1 x 2 x 10'. Illus. 15 shows D,C,E on a 1 x 3 x 10' and a 1 x 3 x 12'. Most 1 x 3 will run about 2½'' or slightly less. To compensate for any difference in lumber size, place each part in position. Drill holes when directions specify same. Only drill hole through adjoining part when same is placed in position. Dash lines on each pattern indicate position of part indicated.

Full size patterns on foldout are A,JA,G,JG,E,SE,F,SF,CA,CC.

17

CUTTING DIAGRAM

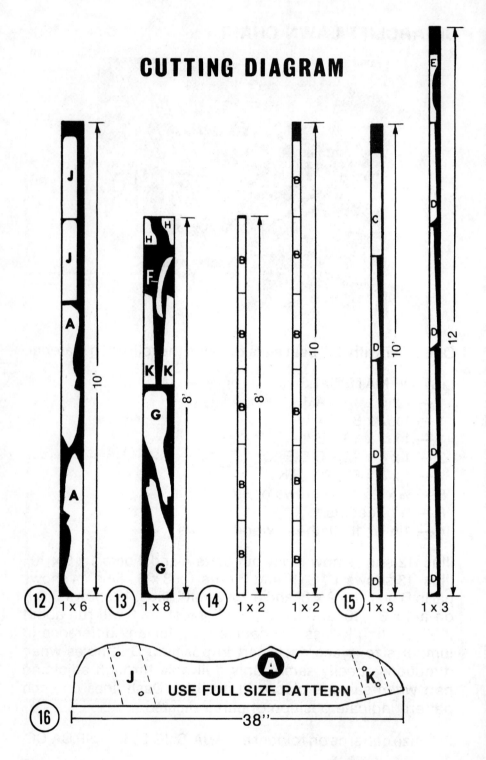

12 1 x 6

13 1 x 8

14 1 x 2   1 x 2   15 1 x 3   1 x 3

16 USE FULL SIZE PATTERN

38"

Cut two seat sides A, Illus. 16, from 1 x 6. Drill two ¼" bolt holes for leg J, and two for back leg K in position shown on pattern.

Cut eleven seat slats B, 1½ x 19", Illus. 17.

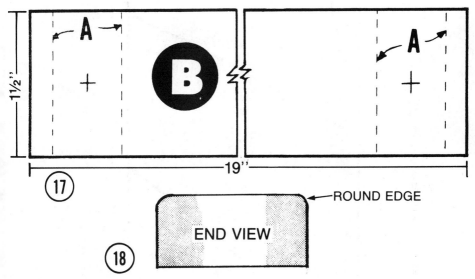

Round top edges to shape shown, Illus. 18.

Cut one front rail C, Illus. 19, 2½ x 19".

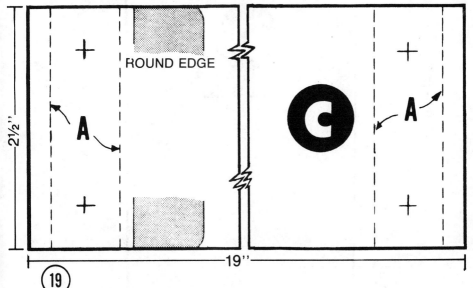

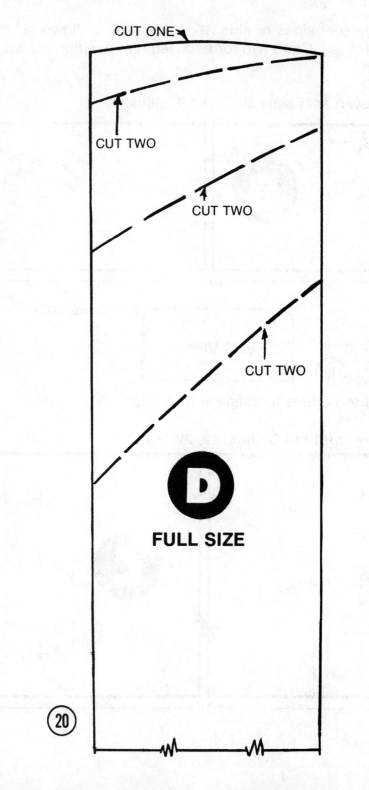

CUT ONE

CUT TWO

CUT TWO

CUT TWO

D

FULL SIZE

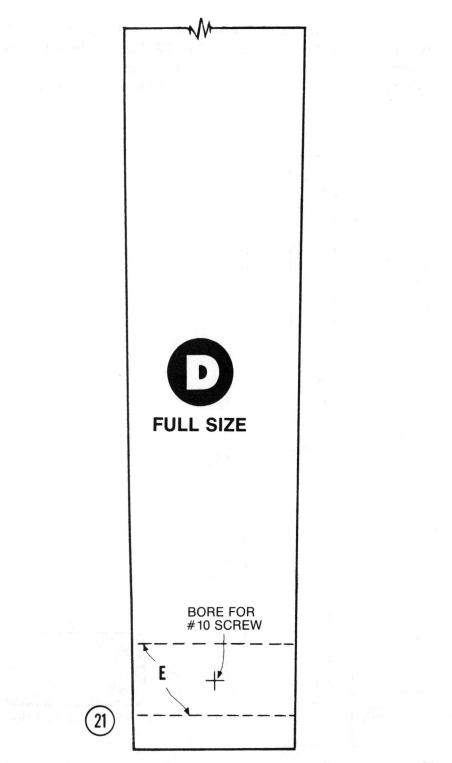

D

FULL SIZE

BORE FOR
#10 SCREW

E

㉑

Illus. 20, 21 show top and bottom ends of D. Cut one 32⅛",
two 32", two 31¼", two 29⅝". Illus. 22 shows overall length
of each slat. Drill hole for #10 screw in position E requires.
Using a file or sandpaper, round four edges to shape shown,
Illus. 23.

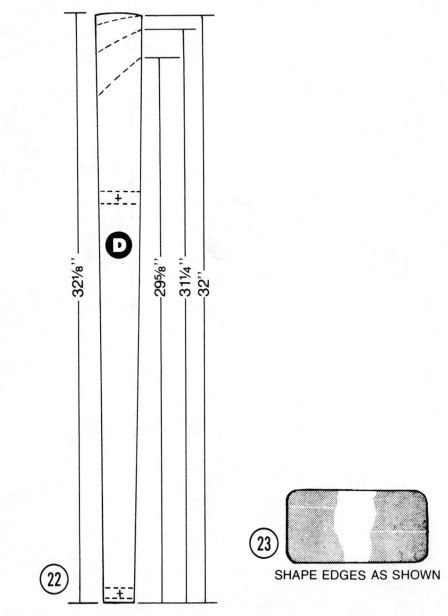

SHAPE EDGES AS SHOWN

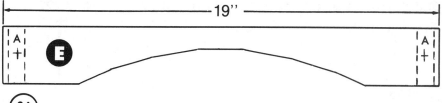

(24)

Cut one lower seat cleat E, Illus. 24, to full size of pattern. Cut E same length as C and B. Place E in position. Drill holes through E where required, Illus. 25.

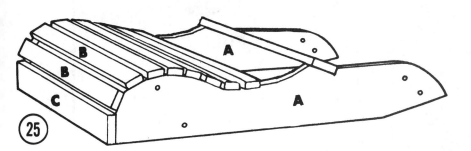

(25)

Cut one upper back cleat F, Illus. 26, to full size of pattern.

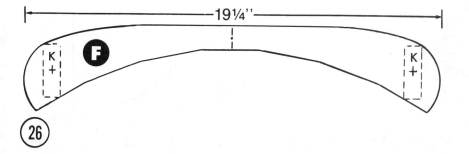

(26)

Cut two arms G to full width of pattern or to width indicated, Illus. 9, 10. Bore holes for #10 screws where full size pattern indicates position of H and J.

23

Cut two arm brackets H to full size of pattern, Illus. 27.

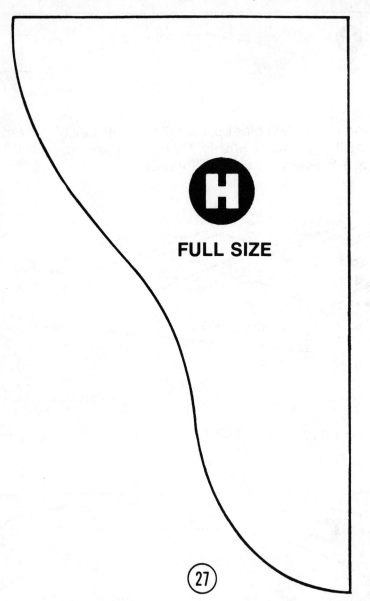

H

FULL SIZE

㉗

Cut two front legs J to overall size shown, Illus. 28. Round four edges, Illus. 23.

Cut two 26" back legs K, Illus. 29. Cut top to angle shown full size, Illus. 30. Drill two ¼" holes at bottom in position shown, Illus. 31.

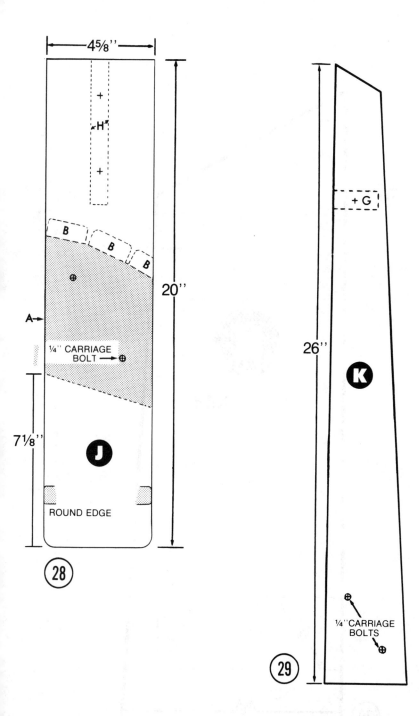

├── 4⅝" ──┤

+

◄H►

+

B

B

B

⊕

A►

¼" CARRIAGE
BOLT ──► ⊕

20"

7⅛"

J

ROUND EDGE

㉘

26"

+ G

K

⊕

¼" CARRIAGE
BOLTS

⊕

㉙

25

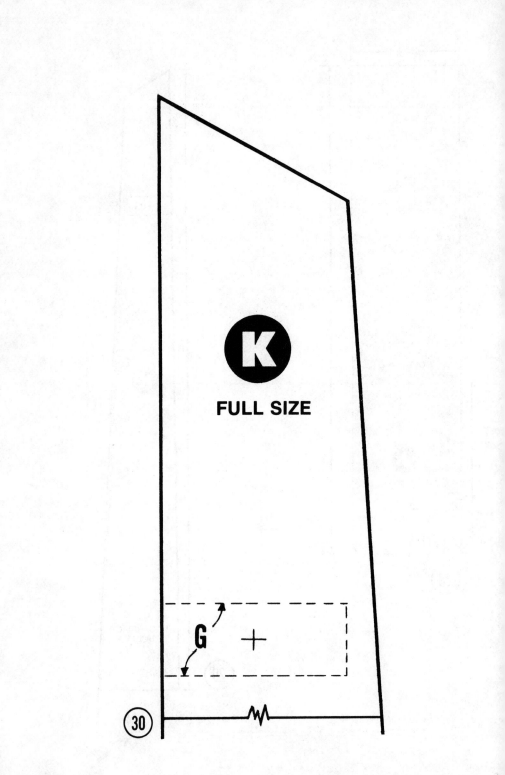

K

FULL SIZE

G +

(30)

26

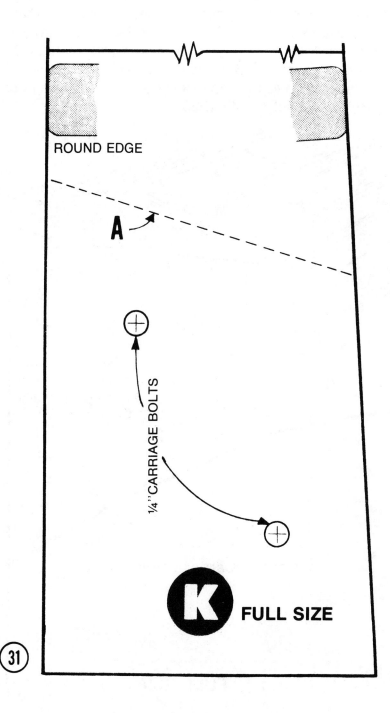

ROUND EDGE

A

¼" CARRIAGE BOLTS

K FULL SIZE

(31)

Apply glue and fasten C and E to A, Illus. 25, with 1½" # 10 flathead brass screws. C and E project ¼" over A. Place assembled frame on a level bench or floor. Check with square. Tack a 1 x 2 brace across A to hold square, Illus. 32. Apply glue and fasten two B to A in position above C. Space B as shown on pattern A. Cut the next three B so they are flush with A, no ¼" projection, Illus. 33.

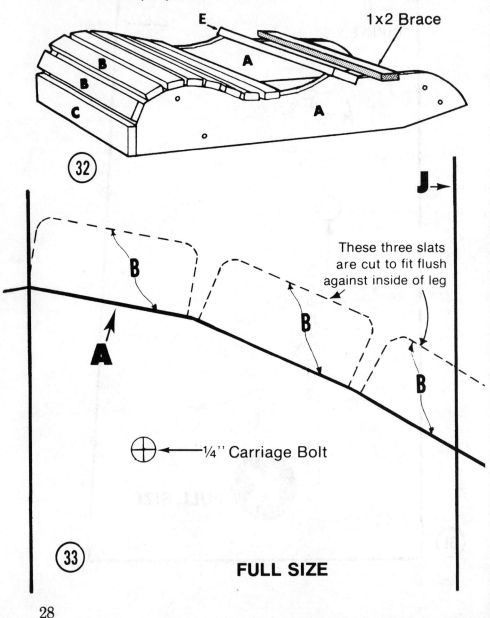

1x2 Brace

E

B

B

A

B

C

A

A

㉜

J→

B

These three slats are cut to fit flush against inside of leg

B

A

B

¼" Carriage Bolt

㉝

FULL SIZE

Drill two screw holes through leg J in position shown, Illus. 28. Fasten J to H with 1½" #10 screws. Clamp A to J, Illus. 34, at height indicated. Check J with level to make certain it's plumb. Insert drill in A, drill through J. Bolt J to A using ¼x2" carriage bolts or ¼" Teenut and 1½" cap screws, Illus. 35.

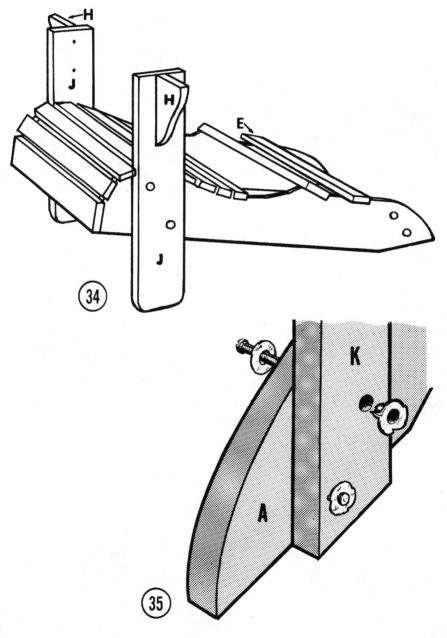

Fasten A to K, Illus. 35, 36, with ¼ x 1½" screws and Teenuts. Position F on K. Drill screw holes through F. Fasten F to K with 2" # 10 screws.

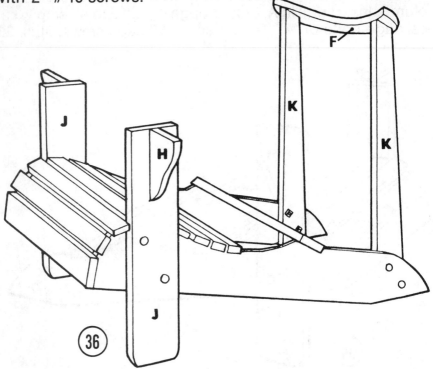

Apply glue to edge of E and F. Fasten 32¼" D in center position to E. Drill hole through D in position F requires. Fasten D to F. Spacing on full size pattern E indicates position of D. Fasten balance of D to E, then create fan shape. When properly positioned, drill shank hole through D and pilot hole in F. Fasten each with 1½" # 10 screws.

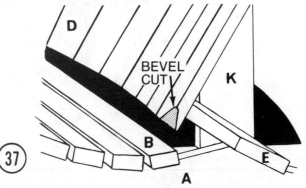

Bevel bottom end of outside D, Illus. 37.

Fasten last three seat slats B in position, Illus. 38. Countersink all screws. Fill holes with wood filler. Sandpaper surface and edges smooth. Paint or stain.

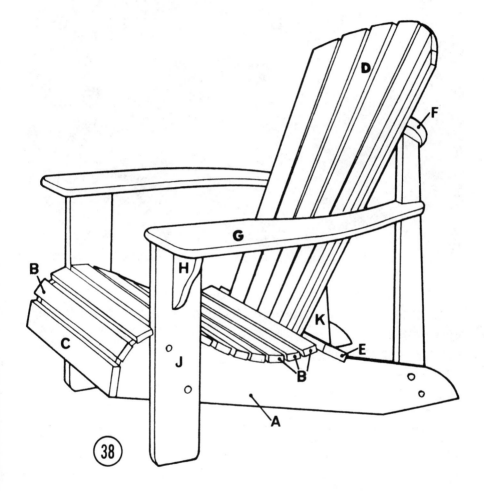

Those building chairs for resale should use Teenuts when fastening J to A and A to K. Use ¼'' Teenuts with ¼ x 1½'' cap screws or roundhead stove bolts. To accommodate barrel of bolt, redrill hole to depth barrel of Teenut requires using a 5/16'' bit. Using a hammer, drive Teenut in position, Illus. 35.

MATCHING SETTEE

A settee, Illus. 2, 39, makes a handsome addition to the chair and table. It can be assembled following the same procedure as a chair.

LIST OF MATERIALS

  2 — 1 x 6 x 10' - A,J,SL
  2 — 1 x 2 x 12' - SB
  1 — 1 x 2 x 14' - SB
  5 — 1 x 4 x 12' - SC,D,SE,SF,SH,K
  1 — 1 x 8 x 8' - G
12 — ¼ x 1½'' Cap Screws or Stove Bolts
12 — ¼'' Teenuts
12 — 2'' #10 flathead wood screws
72 — 1½'' #10 ''   ''   ''

Draw outline of each pattern on lumber specified. Cut three sides A, two legs J. Cut one leg SL to size and shape shown, Illus. 40.

Do not bore bolt holes in legs J, K and SL until you are ready to assemble.

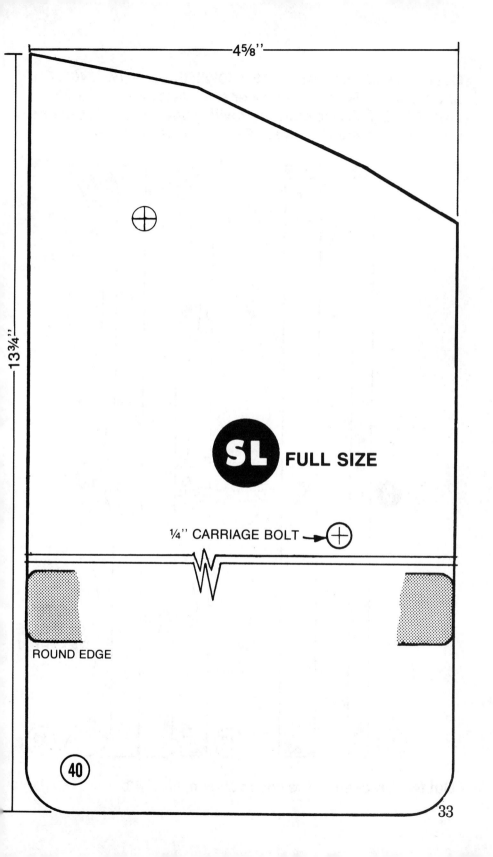

4⅝''

13¾''

SL FULL SIZE

¼'' CARRIAGE BOLT →

ROUND EDGE

㊵

33

Cut eight seat slats SB — 1½ x 40½''; three — 1½ x 40''. Cut one front rail SC and one lower seat cleat SE — 2½ x 40½'', Illus. 41, 42. Full size pattern provides one half of SE. Cut one upper back cleat SF, Illus. 42A, to full size pattern.

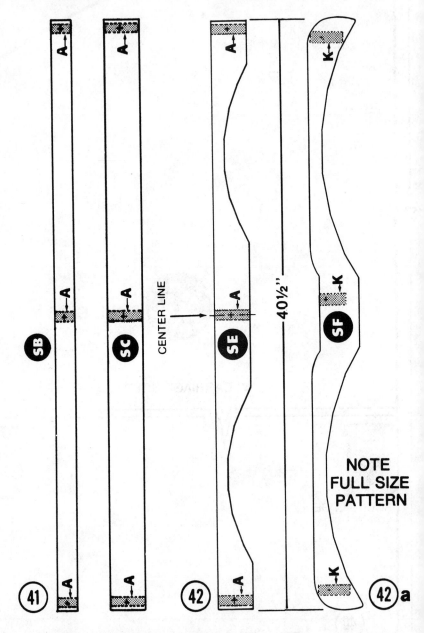

Cut two brackets SH to shape shown, Illus. 43.

Drill ¼'' holes in A where indicated.

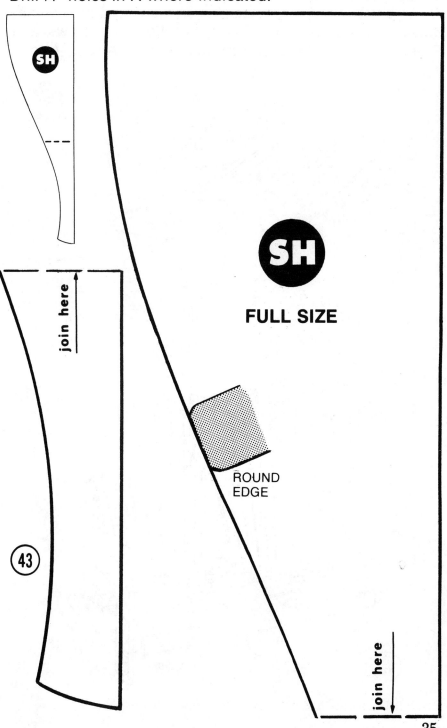

join here

SH

FULL SIZE

ROUND
EDGE

(43)

join here

Clamp J to A in position shown, Illus. 34. Bottom edge of A is 7⅛" from floor. Using holes in A as a guide, drill ¼" holes through J. Fasten J to A with ¼ x 1½" cap screws and Teenuts or roundhead stove bolts. Fasten A to L, A to K, Illus. 44, 45.

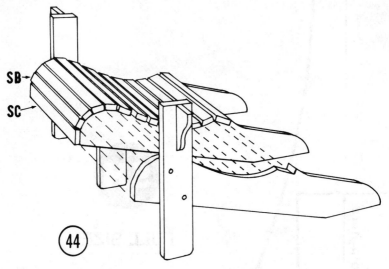

SB

SC

44

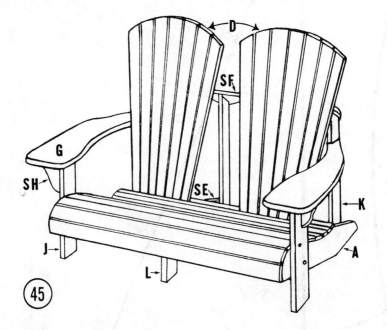

D

SF

G

SH

SE

K

J

A

L

45

Allow leg K to position itself against SF. Drill hole through SF so it can be fastened with a 2'' #10 screw into center of K, Illus. 42, 45.

Fasten arm G to J and SH with 2'' screws, Illus. 46. Screw K to G; D to SE and SF with 1½'' screws. Note position of D on SE and SF. The three seat slats SB that butt against inside face of J are also screwed into top of leg L.

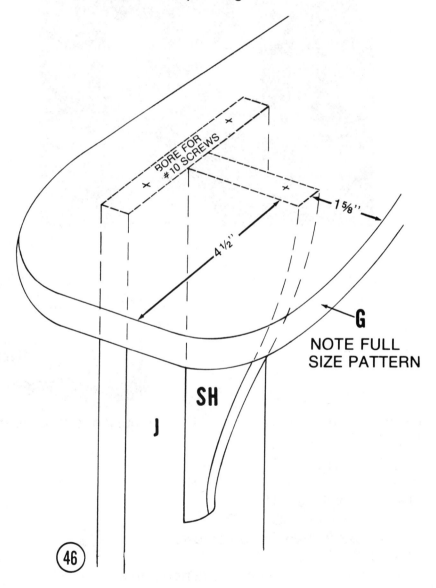

BORE FOR #10 SCREWS

1⅝''

4½''

G

NOTE FULL SIZE PATTERN

SH

J

46

CHILD SIZE CHAIR

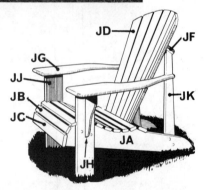

You will need the following materials to build one chair, Illus. 3, 47:

LIST OF MATERIALS
   1 — 1 x 6 x 12' - JA,JE,JF,JG,JK
   1 — 1 x 4 x 4' - JJ,JH
   1 — ½ x 4 x 14' - JB,JC,JD
  34 — 1'' #8 flathead wood screws
  16 — 1½'' #8 ''   ''   ''
   8 — ¼ x 2'' carriage bolts, washers, nuts

The Junior Briarcliff Chair is built following same procedure as the lawn chair. To simplify identification, parts for the Junior Briarcliff Chair have a prefix J. For example JA refers to seat side, JC to front rail, etc., etc.

Shaded area on full size pattern for side A indicates full size JA.

Cut two seat sides JA to full size of shaded area. Drill ¼'' holes in position shown, Illus. 24, 48.

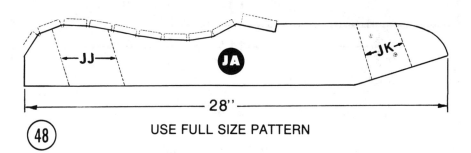

USE FULL SIZE PATTERN

Cut nine seat slats JB, 1½ x 14'', Illus. 49. Round edges as shown, Illus. 18.

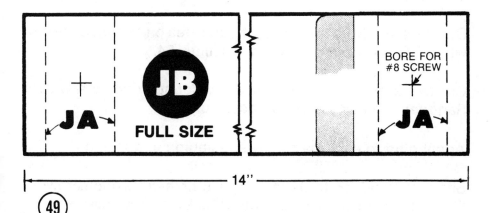

Cut one front seat rail JC, 2 x 14'', Illus. 50. Round top edges as shown.

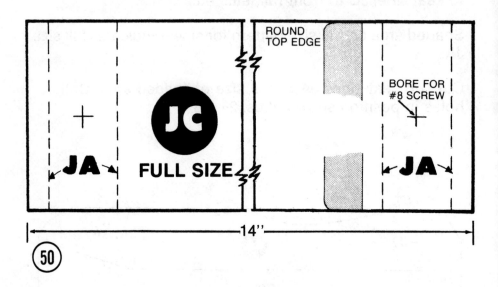

ROUND TOP EDGE

JC FULL SIZE

JA

BORE FOR #8 SCREW

JA

|————————————14''————————————|

(50)

Cut back slats JD to overall length and shape noted, Illus. 51. Round all four edges. Drill hole for #8 screw to fasten JD to JE. Only drill hole for JF after fastening JD to JE.

Cut one lower back cleat JE, Illus. 52. Cut one upper back cleat JF. Illus. 52, 53 provide one half of JE, JF.

Cut two arms JG to full size of shaded area on pattern G. Note where JG is fastened to JH and JJ, Illus. 54.

Cut two arm brackets JH, Illus. 55. Round edge as shown. Sandpaper all edges before assembly.

Apply glue to each part before fastening in position.

Screw JC and JE to JA with 1'' # 8 flathead wood screws. Check to make certain it's square. Tack a 1 x 2 across to hold square, Illus. 32.

40

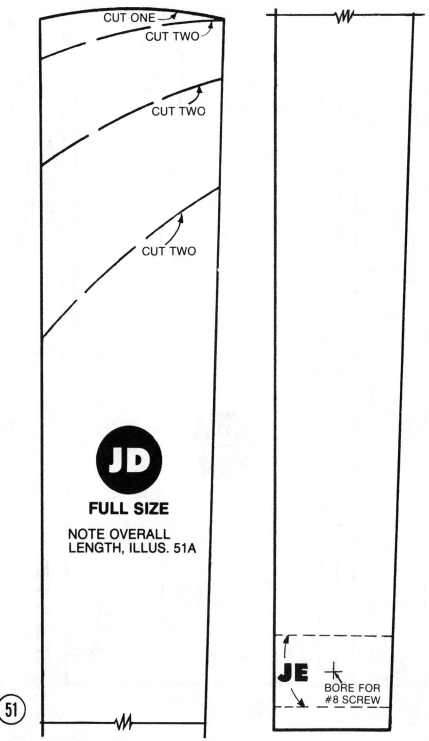

CUT ONE

CUT TWO

CUT TWO

CUT TWO

JD

FULL SIZE

NOTE OVERALL
LENGTH, ILLUS. 51A

(51)

JE

BORE FOR
#8 SCREW

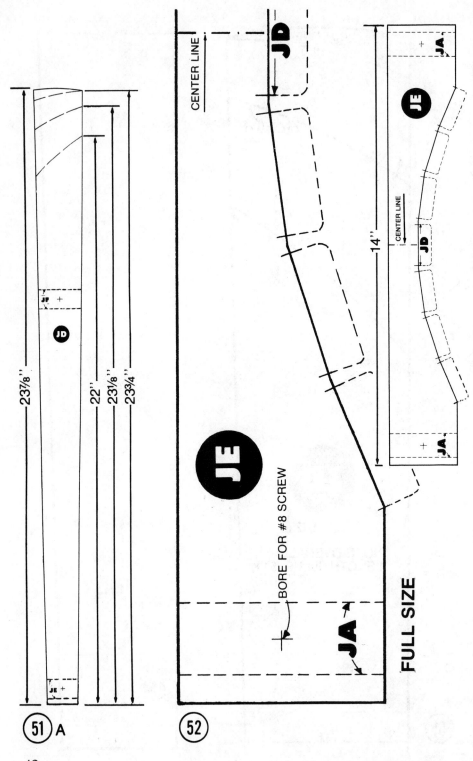

23⅜"

JF +

JD

22"

23⅛"

23¾"

⑤¹ A

JE +

CENTER LINE

JD

JE

BORE FOR #8 SCREW

JA

JA

14"

JA +

JE

CENTER LINE

JD

JA +

FULL SIZE

㊾

42

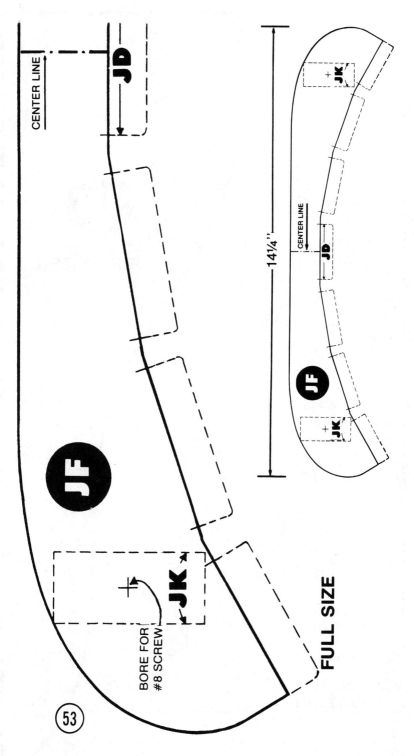

CENTER LINE

JD

JK

JF

14¼"

CENTER LINE

JD

JF

JK

BORE FOR #8 SCREW

JK

FULL SIZE

(53)

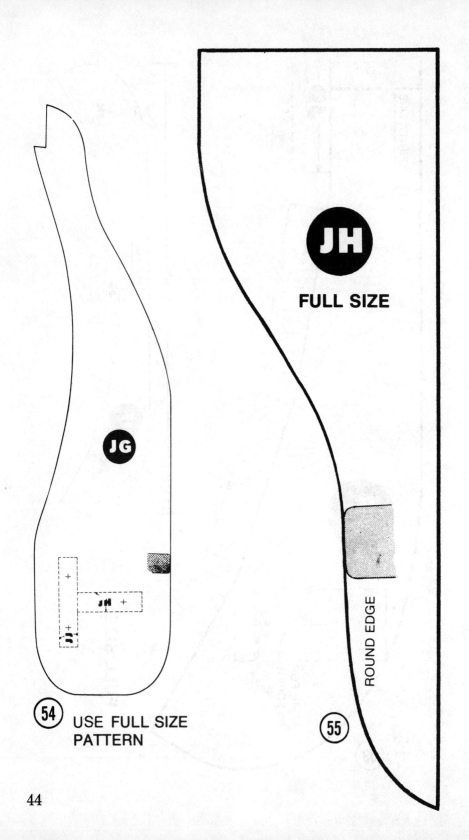

JG

54 USE FULL SIZE PATTERN

JH

FULL SIZE

ROUND EDGE

55

44

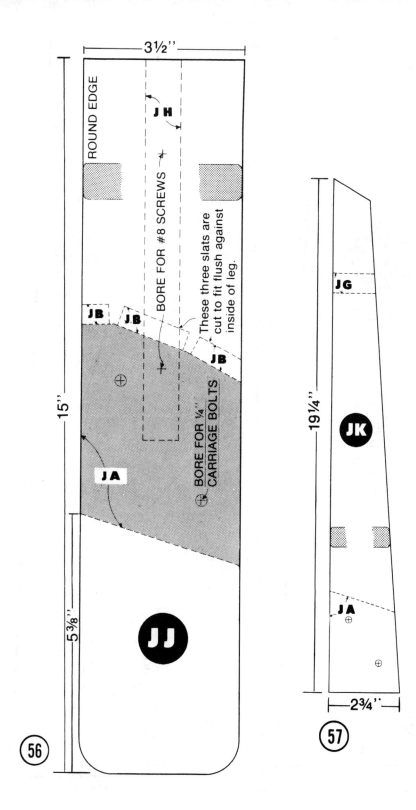

ROUND EDGE

3½"

J H

BORE FOR #8 SCREWS

These three slats are cut to fit flush against inside of leg.

J B   J B

J B

⊕

BORE FOR ¼" CARRIAGE BOLTS
⊕

J A

15"

5⅜"

JJ

⑤⑥

J G

JK

19¼"

J A
⊕

⊕

2¾"

⑤⑦

45

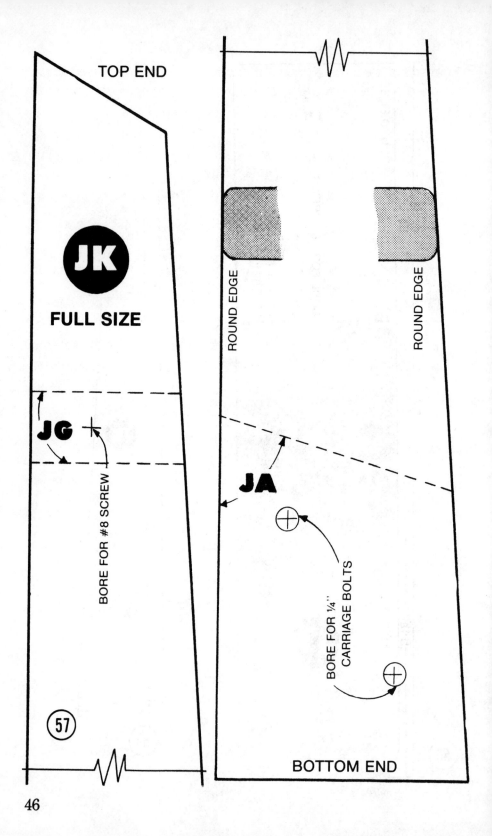

TOP END

JK

FULL SIZE

JG

BORE FOR #8 SCREW

(57)

ROUND EDGE

ROUND EDGE

JA

BORE FOR ¼"
CARRIAGE BOLTS

BOTTOM END

Fasten slats JB to JA with the exception of the last three slats. The slats that butt against leg JJ must be sawed flush with face of JA.

Fasten leg JJ, Illus. 56, to JH with 1½" screws. Cut two JK, Illus. 57. Clamp JJ and JK temporarily to JA. Using holes through JA as a guide, bore ¼" holes through JJ and JK. Bolt JJ and JK to JA with ¼ x 1½" cap screws and Teenuts or use ¼ x 2" carriage bolts, nuts and washers, Illus. 35.

Fasten JF to JK with 1½" screws.

Fasten center slat JD to JE and JF with 1" screws, then fasten other JD in position shown.

Fasten JG to JJ and JH and JK to JG with 1½" screws.

Bevel lower outside end of JD, Illus. 37. Fasten last three seat slats JB in position. Countersink all screws, fill holes with wood filler. Sandpaper entire chair. Apply a coat of primer or wood preservative before painting with exterior paint.

ROUND TOP TABLE

This easy to build table, Illus. 4, 58, 58A, complements the chair, settee and lounge. Use only exterior grade plywood.

LIST OF MATERIALS
1 — ¾ x 4'' x 4' exterior plywood
8 — 1½'' #10 flathead wood screws
4 — ⅜ x 2'' carriage bolts, washers, wing nuts*

Those who prefer a bit more design can cut 2'' holes in the legs, Illus. 58A.

*Or use ⅜'' Teenuts and ⅜ x 1½'' cap screws.

Illus. 59 shows how to position and cut parts from a ¾ x 4 x 4' panel of exterior plywood. An easy way to draw A is to drive an 8 penny finishing nail about 1" from the end of a 1 x 2 x 24", Illus. 59A. Drill a ¼" hole, 16½" from nail. Place pencil through hole. Tack nail to plywood in position shown and scribe a circle. Use a saber or compass saw to cut top.

CUTTING DIAGRAM

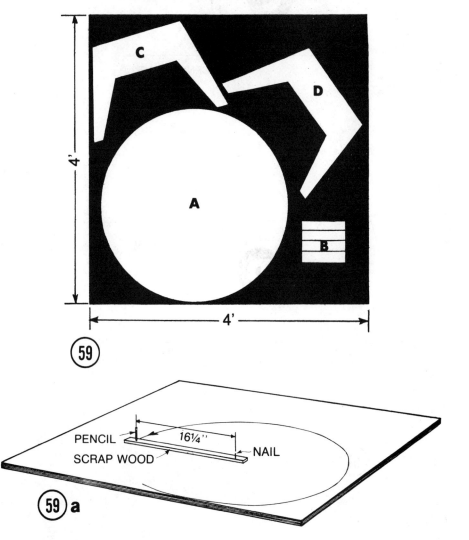

Pages 51, 52, 53 provide a full size pattern for half of leg C and D. Join where indicated, Illus. 60. Draw a ¾ x 3'' slot in leg C in position shown.

Draw a matching slot in leg D in position shown, Illus. 61. Cut both slots to exact thickness of plywood used.

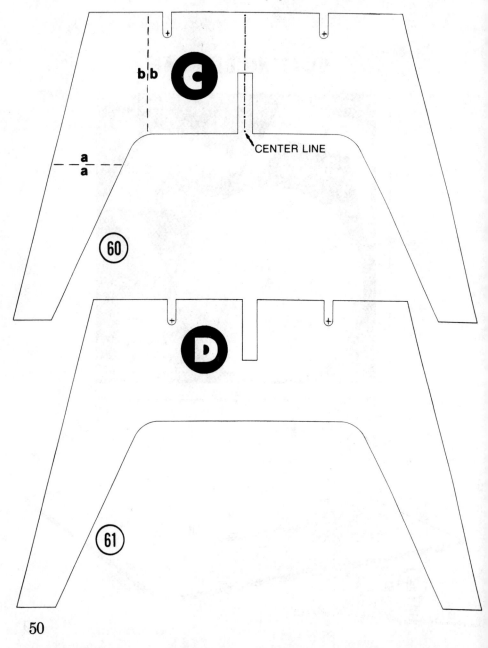

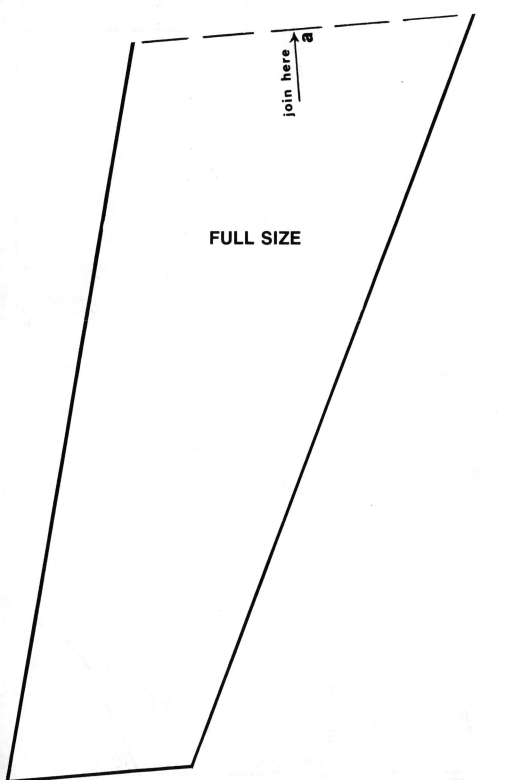

join here ↑ a

FULL SIZE

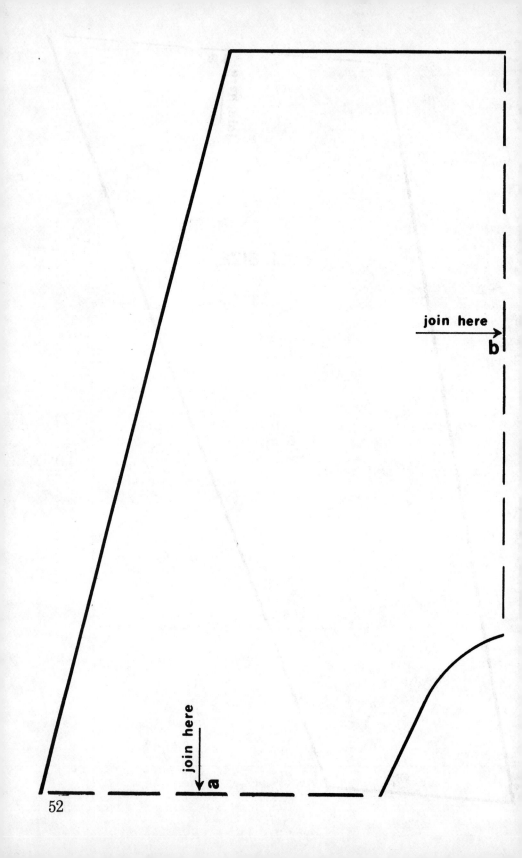

join here
→
b

join here
↓
a

52

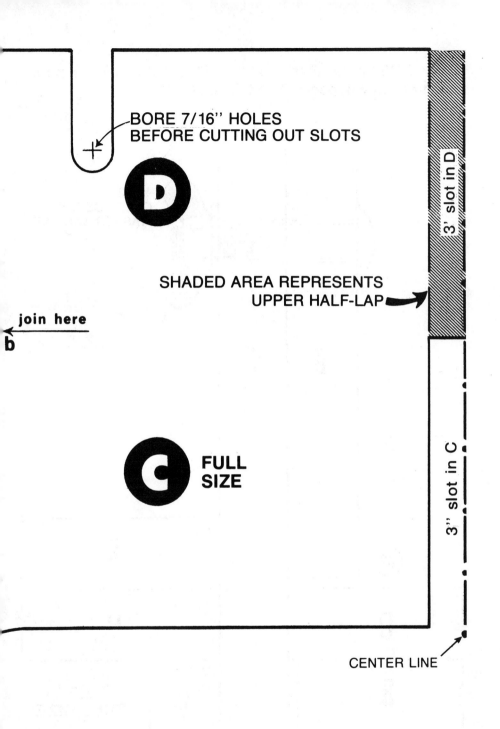

BORE 7/16" HOLES
BEFORE CUTTING OUT SLOTS

D

3' slot in D

SHADED AREA REPRESENTS
UPPER HALF-LAP

join here

b

C FULL SIZE

3" slot in C

CENTER LINE

Bore 7/16'' hole, then saw two 7/16 x 1¼'' deep slots in position shown, page 50 and Illus. 60, 61.

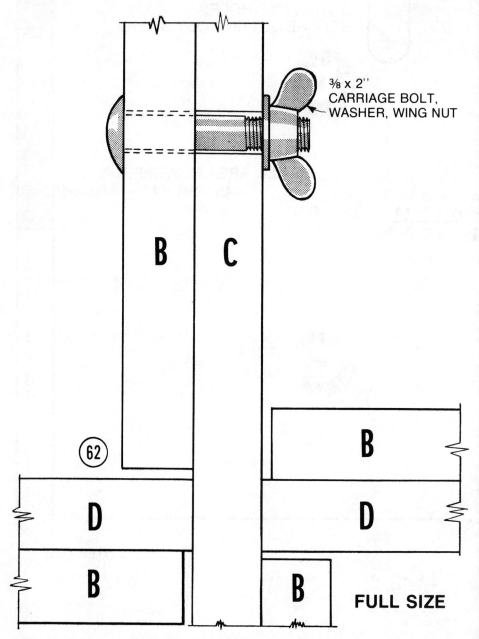

⅜ x 2''
CARRIAGE BOLT,
WASHER, WING NUT

B C

62

B

D   D

B   B

FULL SIZE

Those who want to cut 2''holes in legs, Illus. 58A, should draw a line 1'' in from outside edge of leg at bottom, 2¾'' in at top,

Illus. 64. Measure up 4¾, 4, 4" and mark leg. Use an expansion bit, Illus. 65, to bore three 2" holes in each leg.

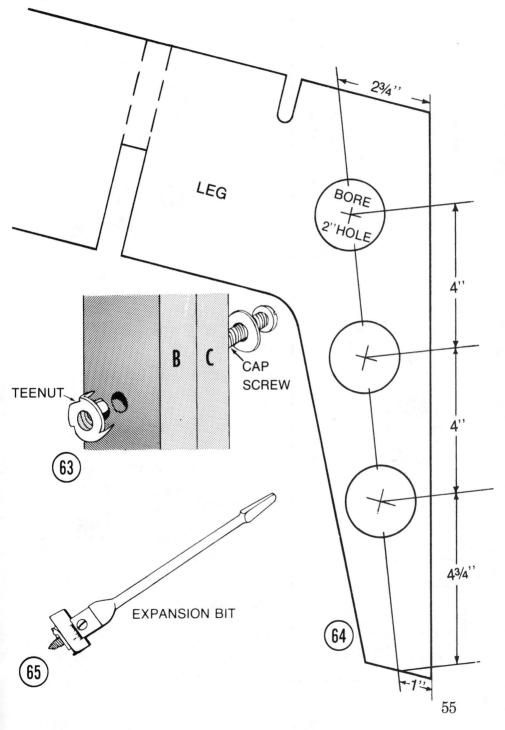

LEG

2¾"

BORE 2"HOLE

4"

4"

4¾"

1"

B C

CAP SCREW

TEENUT

63

EXPANSION BIT

65

64

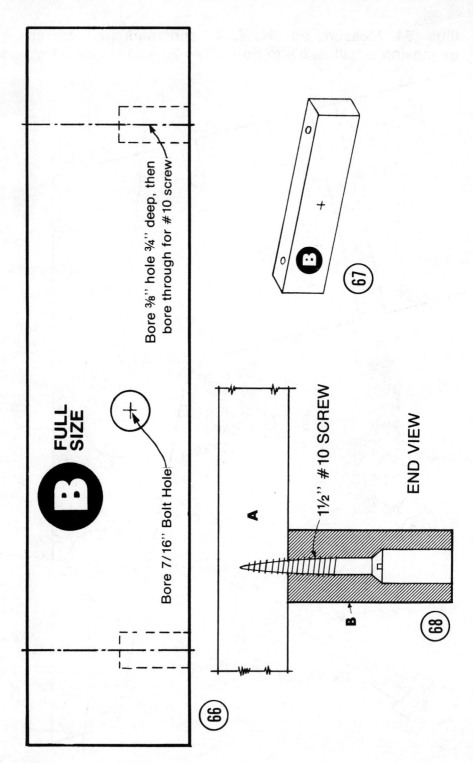

FULL SIZE

B

Bore 7/16" Bolt Hole

Bore 3/8" hole 3/4" deep, then bore through for #10 screw

66

67

B

A

1½" #10 SCREW

B

68

END VIEW

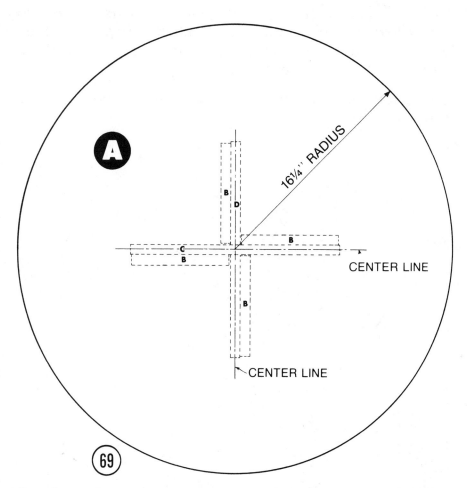

CENTER LINE

16¼" RADIUS

CENTER LINE

(69)

Cut four cleats B, ¾ x 1¾ x 7½", Illus. 66. Bore 7/16" hole through B in position shown. Bore two ⅜" holes, ¾" deep through edge of each B, Illus. 67. Continue drilling a 3/32" pilot hole. This permits gluing and screwing cleat B to A with 1½" # 10 screws, Illus. 68.

Draw center lines across bottom face of A, Illus. 69.

Join legs C and D together, Illus. 70. Place A bottom face up on a level surface. Toenail legs temporarily in position shown. Place cleats B in position shown. Check to make certain bolt hole in B lines up with slot in C and D. When these check out OK, apply glue to edge of B. Fasten B to A with 1½" screws. When B is fastened in place, pull nails and remove C and D. This prevents glue from fastening legs to top. Allow glue to set full time manufacturer specifies, then assemble table using ⅜ x 2" carriage bolts, or ⅜" Teenuts with ⅜ x 1½" cap screws, Illus. 63.

Sandpaper all edges and surfaces before painting with wood preservative.

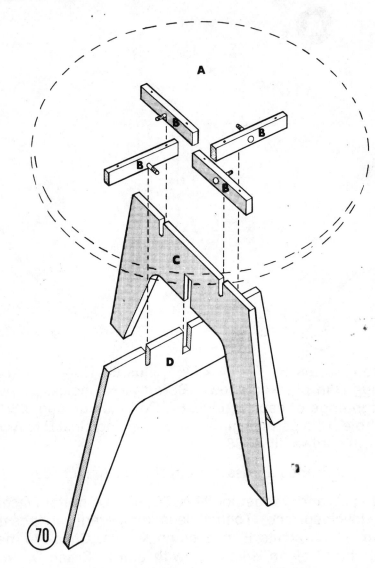

EASY TO BUILD CHAISE

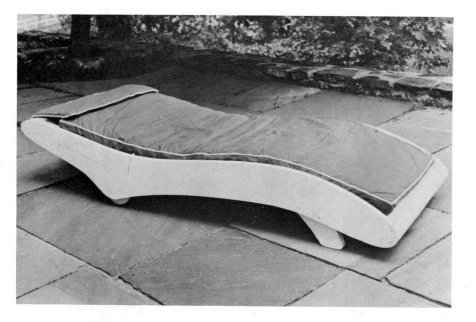

Sleek, smooth, superbly comfortable are but a few of the words used to describe this chaise on wheels. Its size permits covering with a 30 x 75" cot mattress. A 2 to 3" foam rubber pad, covered in water repellant fabric can also be used. Like all the furniture, the chaise is easy to build.

The three position adjustable back rest encourages sunning, sitting and sleeping. When a colorful sailcloth covered pad is positioned on the handsome white frame, you become the proud owner of one of the finest pieces of outdoor furniture available.

If you live in an area where it's still possible to obtain 5/4 x 12" lumber, at a price you can afford, buy it. It's perfect for this chaise. 1 x 12" or ¾" exterior grade plywood could be substituted in place of the 5/4" stock. Use pine, Phillipine mahogany or redwood.

Read directions through completely before starting construction.

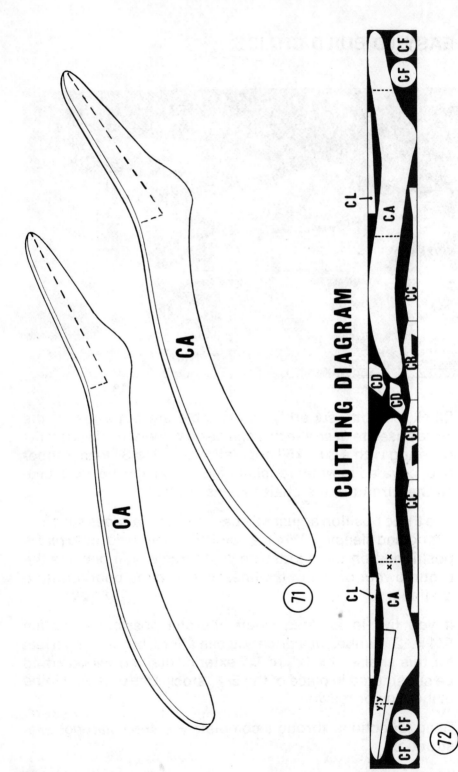

CA

CA

71

CUTTING DIAGRAM

CF CF

CL

CA

CC

CD CD

CB

CR

CB

CC

CL

CA

x¦x

y¦y

CF

CF CF

72

LIST OF MATERIALS
1 — 5/4 x 12 x 14' - CA,CB,CC,CD,CF,CL
1 — 2 x 4 x 8' - CK,CM,CO
4 — 1 x 4 x 8' - CJ
1 — 1 x 4 x 3' - CN
1 — 1 x 2 x 8' - CP,CQ
1 - 1⅜" x 3' oak clothespole - CE
¼ and ⅜" scrap exterior grade plywood - CG,CH
4 — ⅜ x 3" carriage bolts, nuts, washers
2 — ¼ x 2¼"   "   "   "   "   or
4 — ⅜" Teenuts and ⅜ x 2½" cap screws
2 — ¼" Teenuts and ¼ x 1¾" cap screws
74 — 1½" #10 flathead screws
72 — 2" #10   "   "
1 box brads
1 pr. 1 3/32 x 6" (open size) strap hinges

The pattern CA, Illus. 71, is in three parts. Join at X and Y to make a one piece pattern. Lay out parts on a 5/4 x 12, 1 x 12 or ¾" x 4 x 8' exterior grade plywood. Cut two CA, two CB, two CC, two CD, four CF, two CL, Illus. 72.

After cutting two CA to full size of pattern, Illus. 71, recut CA along long dash lines — — —. The two 4 x 27¾" pieces provide the frame for the back rest, Illus. 73, 92.

Bore ¼" hole through A for carriage bolt. Bore hole for axle to size axle requires. We show a 1⅜" hole, Illus. 73, 79, for axle CE. Drill a 3/16" shank hole in position shown, through edge of CA for a 1½" No. 10 screw. This screw locks axle in position. Do not bore other screw holes at this time.

Cut two cleats CB, Illus. 74, and two CC, Illus. 75, to full size of pattern. Bore 3/16" shank holes for #10 screws in position shown.

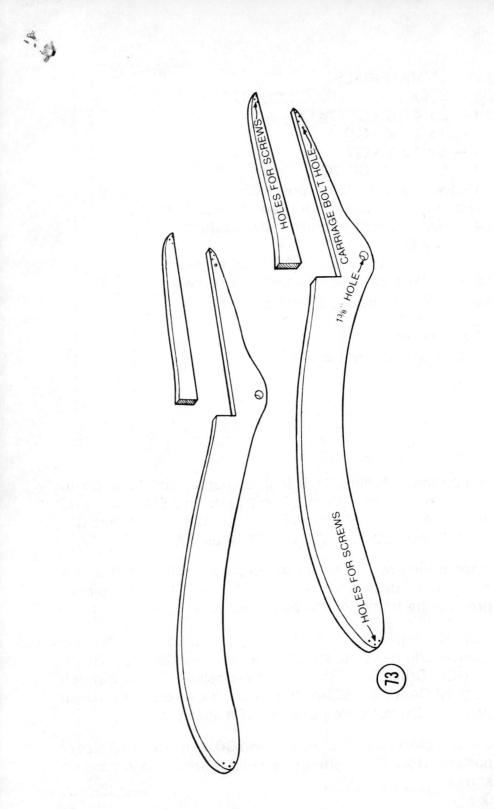

HOLES FOR SCREWS

CARRIAGE BOLT HOLE

$1\frac{3}{8}$" HOLE

HOLES FOR SCREWS

73

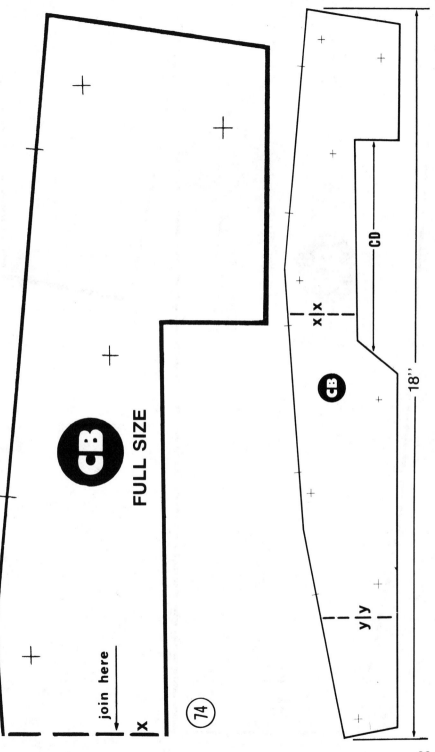

FULL SIZE

CB

join here

x

74

CB

x|x

CD

18"

y|y

63

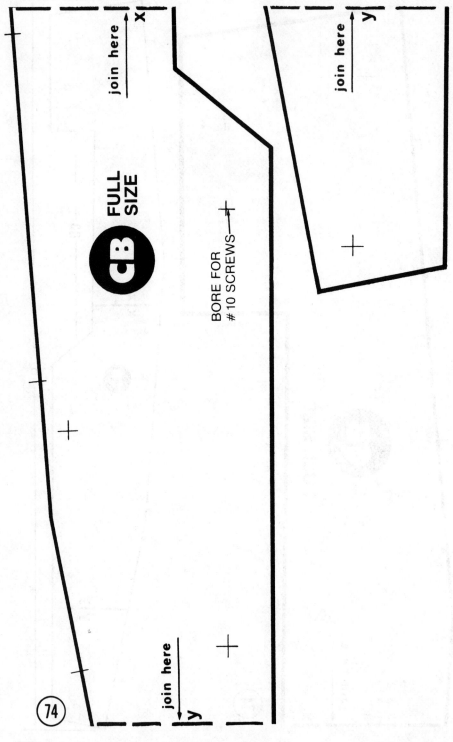

FULL SIZE

join here →x

join here →y

join here →y

BORE FOR
#10 SCREWS→+

74

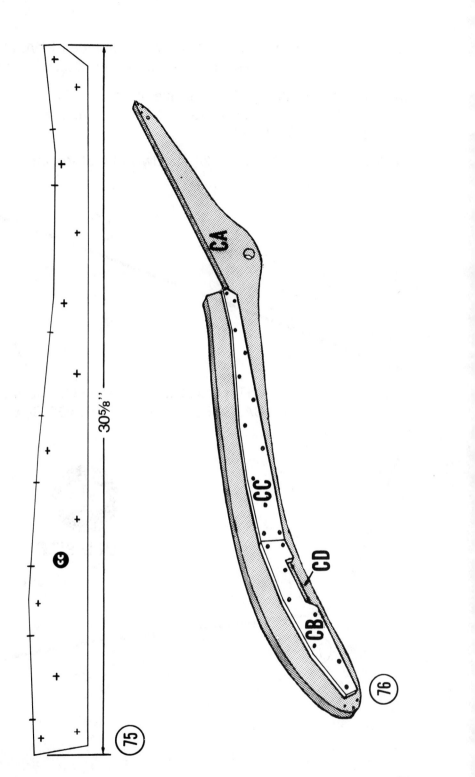

30⅝"

CA

CC

CD

CB

75

76

65

Apply glue and fasten CB and CC to inside face of CA, Illus. 76, using 2" #10 screws. Note position on full size pattern.

Cut two legs CD, Illus. 77, to full size of pattern. Clamp CD to inside face of CA in exact position shown on pattern. Drill ⅜" holes through CD and CA.

Cut a 32½" axle CE from 1⅜" hardwood clothespole.

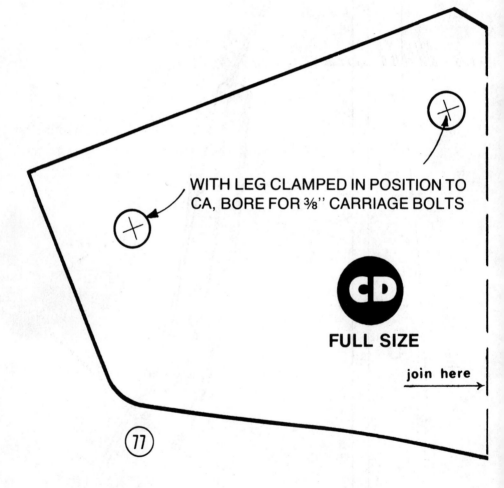

WITH LEG CLAMPED IN POSITION TO CA, BORE FOR ⅜" CARRIAGE BOLTS

CD

FULL SIZE

join here

⑦⑦

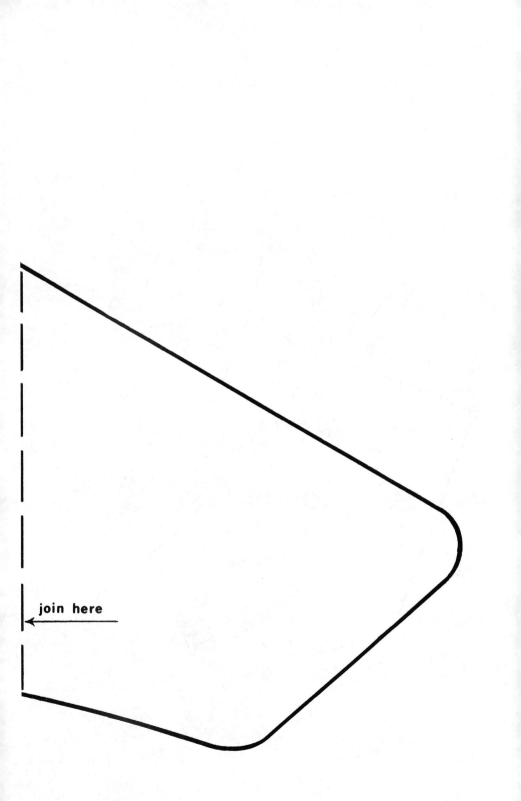

join here

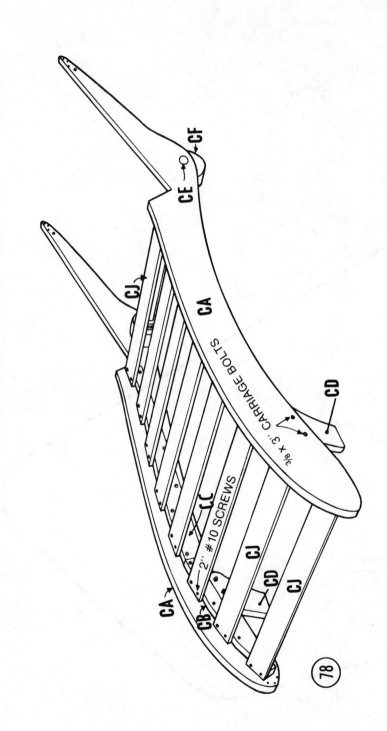

CF

CE

CJ

CA

CD

⅜" X 3" CARRIAGE BOLTS

CC

2" #10 SCREWS

CA

CJ

CD

CB

CJ

78

68

Cut four 6'' wheels, CF, Illus. 79. Bore hole at center for axle.

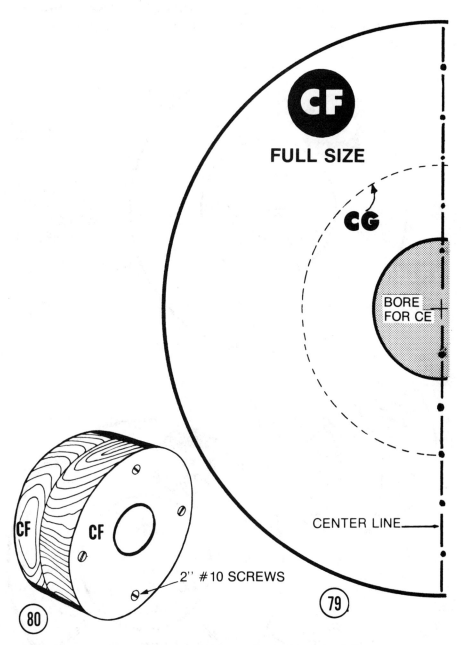

CF

FULL SIZE

CG

BORE
FOR CE

CENTER LINE

CF   CF

2'' #10 SCREWS

⑧⓪

⑦⑨

To form a 2¼'' thick wheel, glue and screw two CF together
using four 2'' #10 screws, Illus. 80. Position pieces so grain
in each piece runs in opposite directions.

69

Cut four wheel washers, CG, Illus. 81, from ¼" exterior grade plywood. Glue and nail CG to both sides of CF. Use 1" brads, Illus. 82. Bore hole for axle through washers. Wheels must turn freely on axle.

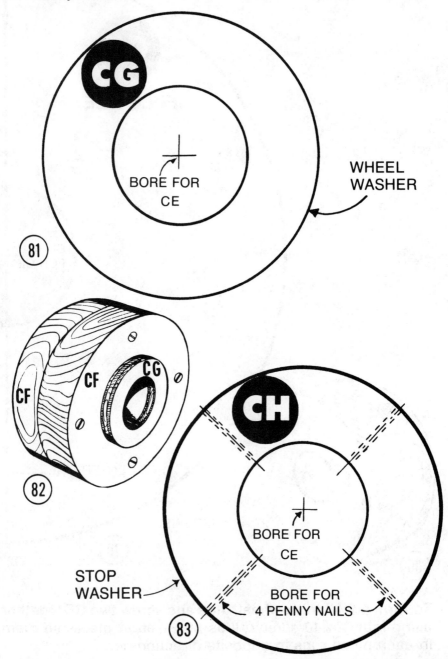

CG

BORE FOR CE

WHEEL WASHER

81

CF   CF   CG

82

CH

BORE FOR CE

STOP WASHER

BORE FOR 4 PENNY NAILS

83

Cut four stop washers CH, Illus. 83, from ⅜" exterior grade plywood. Bore hole for axle. Bore four holes through edge of CH in position indicated to permit driving 4 penny nails without splitting CH.

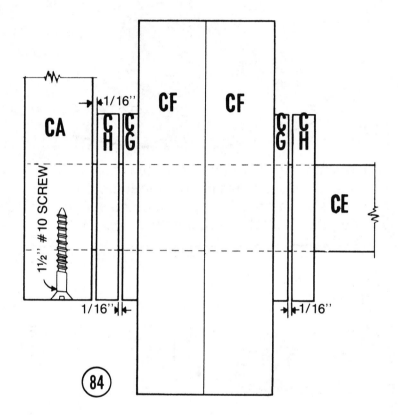

Paint axle, wheels and washers before assembling in place. When dry, insert CE through CA. Place a CH and a wheel, Illus. 84, two more CH and a wheel, another CH. Then slide CE into CA. Axle finishes flush with CA on both sides, Illus. 78.

Lock CE in position with the 1½" # 10 screw through edge of CA, Illus. 85. Allow 1/16" spacing shown, Illus. 84. Fasten CH to CE by driving the four 4 penny nails in position, Illus. 83. Be sure to maintain the 1/16" clearance.

71

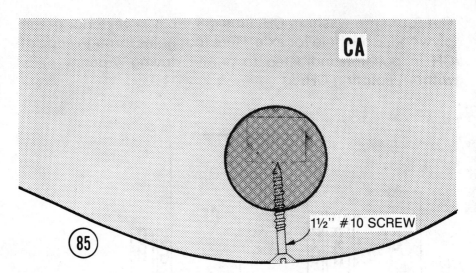

CA

1½" #10 SCREW

85

Cut twelve slats CJ, Illus. 86, 3½ x 30¼" from 1 x 4. Bore shank holes for #10 screws in position indicated. Location of each CJ is shown on CA. Apply glue and screw CJ to CB and CC with 1½" #10 flathead screws, Illus. 78.

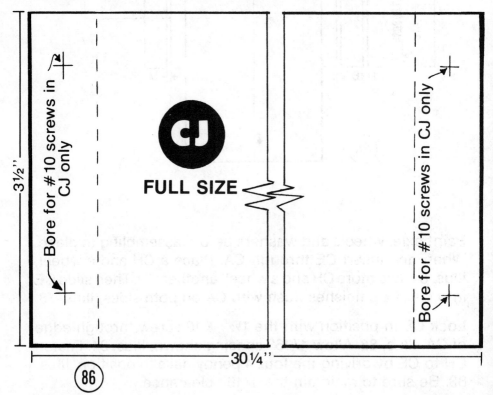

3½"

Bore for #10 screws in CJ only

CJ

FULL SIZE

Bore for #10 screws in CJ only

30¼"

86

Bolt CD to inside face of CA with ⅜ x 3" carriage bolts.

Cut CK from 2 x 4 x 30¼". Note position of CK, Illus. 87, 88. Using a ripsaw, make sawcut indicated by dash lines. You can now plane, file or Surform to shape required. Sandpaper to finish surface. Apply glue and fasten CA to CK in position shown with 2" #10 screws. Note position of screw holes, Illus. 87.

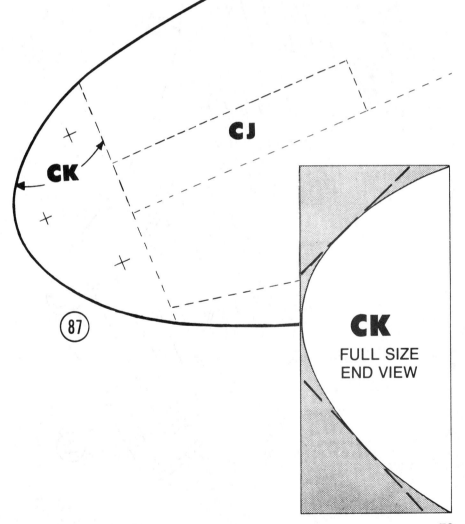

CA

CJ

CK

(87)

CK
FULL SIZE
END VIEW

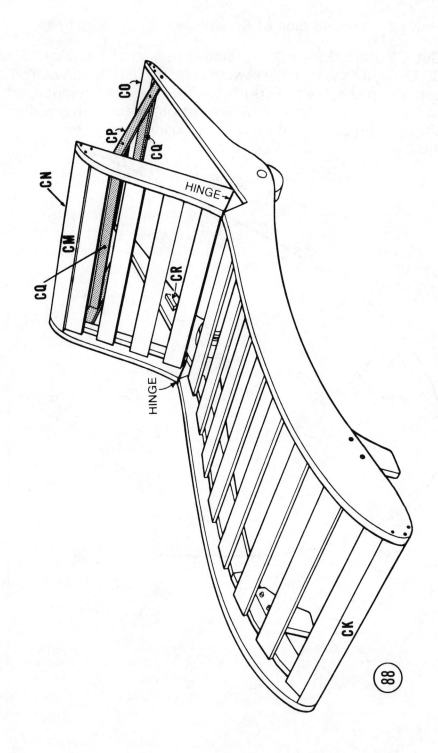

CO
CP
CQ
CN
CM
CQ
HINGE
CR
HINGE
CK
88

74

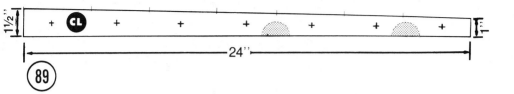

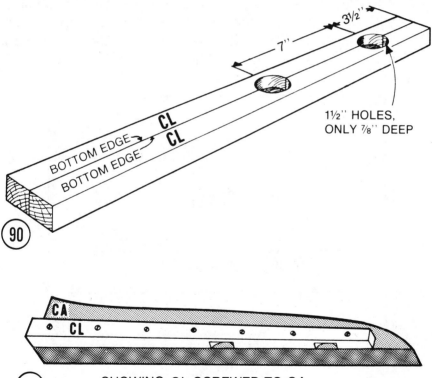

Cut two cleats CL, Illus. 89. CL is 1½" at one end, 1" at other, 24" long. Clamp two pieces together, or temporarily nail same to a board, Illus. 90, in position shown. Bore two 1½" holes ⅞" deep (through 5/4" stock). Remove clamp. Bore through CL for #10 screws in position indicated. Apply glue and fasten CL to cutout from A, Illus. 91, 92, in position shown on full size pattern CA, using 2" #10 screws. The half circles bored in edge of CL receive end of CP, Illus. 88.

SHOWING CL SCREWED TO CA
NOTE POSITION OF 1½" HOLES

75

Glue and screw four slats CJ to CL with 1½'' #10 screws, Illus. 92.

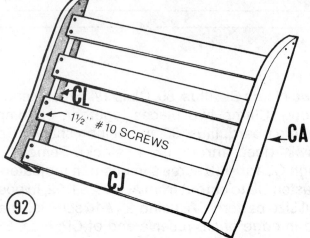

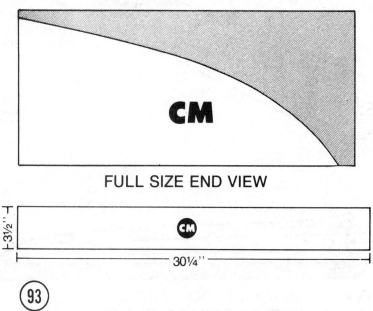

Cut end CM 30¼'' from 2 x 4. Note shape shown in full size end view, Illus. 93. Saw, plane and sandpaper to shape. Place CM in position. Drill shank holes through CA in position shown, Illus. 92. Apply glue and fasten CA to CM with 2'' #10 screws.

CM

FULL SIZE END VIEW

3½''

CM

30¼''

93

Cut handle cleat CN, Illus. 94, 1 x 4 x 30¼". Shape top edge, Illus. 95. Bore four shank holes in position shown for #10 screws. Saw 1 x 4 notch in top edge, Illus. 96. Apply glue and fasten CN to CM with four 1½" #10 screws. Nail through CM into CN with 4 penny nails spaced about 4" apart. Fasten CA to CN with 2" #10 screws.

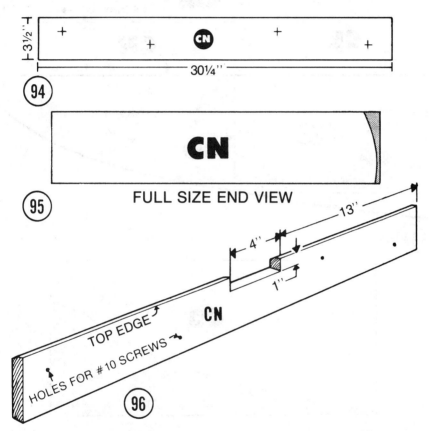

FULL SIZE END VIEW

Cut 2 x 4 x 30¼" CO to shape shown, Illus. 98. Apply glue and screw CA to CO with 2" screws, Illus. 97.

Cut two back supports CP, 1 x 2 x 18", Illus. 99. Bore hole for ¼" carriage bolt, also for #10 screw where indicated. Round ends to shape shown.

Cut two cross braces CQ, 1 x 2 x 28⅝", Illus. 100. Glue and screw CP to CQ in position shown, Illus. 99, using 1½" #10 screws.

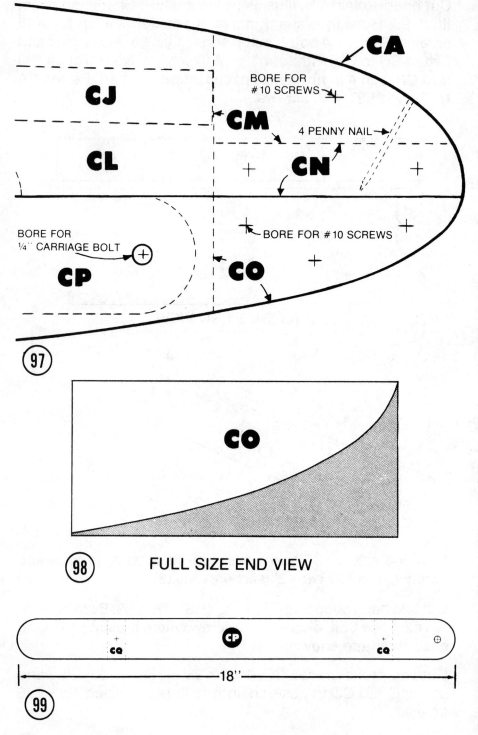

BORE FOR #10 SCREWS

CA

CJ

CM

4 PENNY NAIL

CL

CN

BORE FOR 1/4" CARRIAGE BOLT

CP

CO

BORE FOR #10 SCREWS

(97)

CO

(98) FULL SIZE END VIEW

CP

cq

cq

|←————— 18" —————→|

(99)

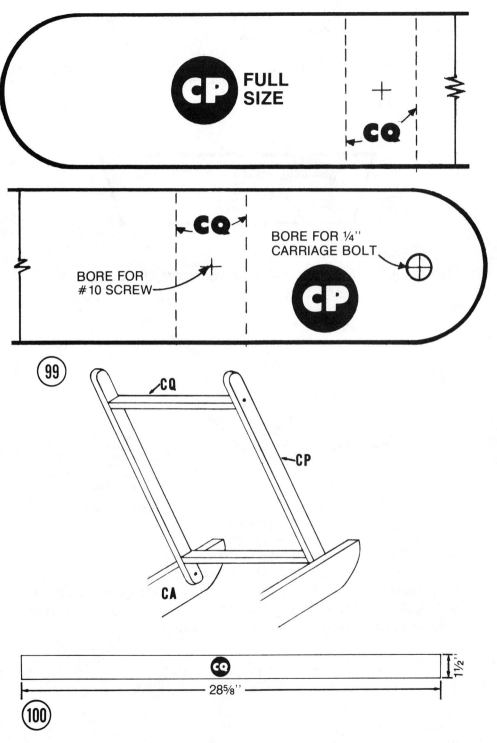

CP FULL SIZE

CQ

BORE FOR
#10 SCREW

CQ

BORE FOR ¼''
CARRIAGE BOLT

CP

(99)

CQ

CP

CA

CQ

1½''

28⅝''

(100)

Bolt CA to CP with ¼ x 2¼" carriage bolts. Place a washer between CA and CP, Illus. 88.

Cut two stops CR, Illus. 88, 101, from 1 x 2. Glue and nail CR to inside face of CA with 4 penny nails in position shown on full size pattern CA.

Fasten strap hinges to CA and back rest, Illus. 102.

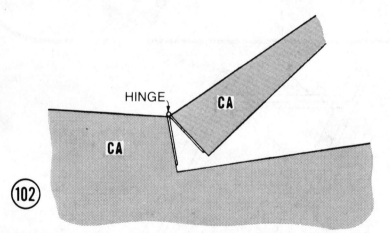

Countersink all nailheads and screws. Fill holes with woodfiller. Sandpaper all surfaces and edges smooth. Prime with wood preservative. Paint with exterior grade paint or semigloss enamel. Buy a cover for a 2 or 3", 30 x 75" foam rubber pad or sew a water repellant cover.

PICNIC TABLE

The fun of dining out takes on a new meaning when you have this 4 x 6' picnic table in your own backyard, Illus. 103. To lengthen its lifespan, seats and top fold back when not in use. Simplified construction permits building an eight or ten foot length. Take-apart sections permit winter storage in a minimum of space.

LIST OF MATERIALS
    1 — 2 x 10 x 12' - A
    2 — 1 x 10 x 12' - B (or 2 x 10 x 12')
    1 — 1 x 6 x 6' - D
    1 — 1 x 3 x 6'
    1 — 1 x 3 x 10' - J,K,L
    1 — 2 x 3 x 10'
    1 — 2 x 3 x 12' - C,G,H
    1 — 2 x 4 x 12' - E
    1 — 2 x 6 x 4' - F
  20 — 3" #12 flathead screws
  16 — 1¾" #10 "   "
  64 — 1¼" #10 "   "
    5 — ½ x 4" carriage bolts, nuts, washers
    8 — ⅜ x 8"   "   "   "   "
    4 — 5/16 x 4" hanger bolts, nuts, washers

81

CUTTING DIAGRAM

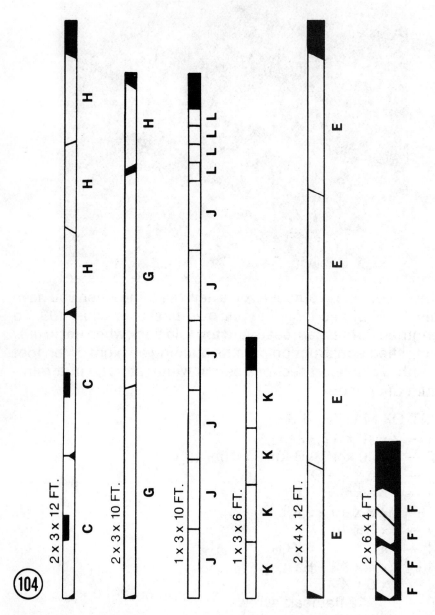

Illus. 104 provides a cutting diagram.

Cut two seats A, 2 x 10 x 6', Illus. 105.

Cut four top boards B, 1 x 10 x 6', Illus. 106.

82

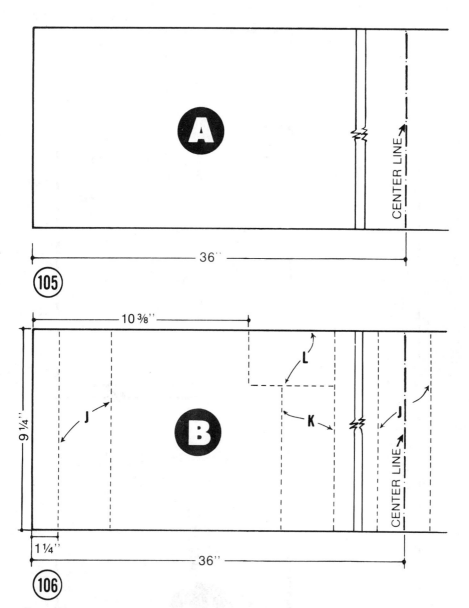

Cut two leg cleats C, 2 x 3 x 32½", Illus. 107.

Illus. 108 shows full size angle at both ends. Saw a ¾" deep by 5" long notch in position shown. Make two ¾" saw cuts 2½" from center line, Illus. 109. Use a ¾ or 1" chisel to cut notch ¾ x 5" at center. Bore a 5/16" hole through C — 13/16" from center line, Illus. 110. Bore four 7/32" shank holes for 3" #12 screws, Illus. 107, 111.

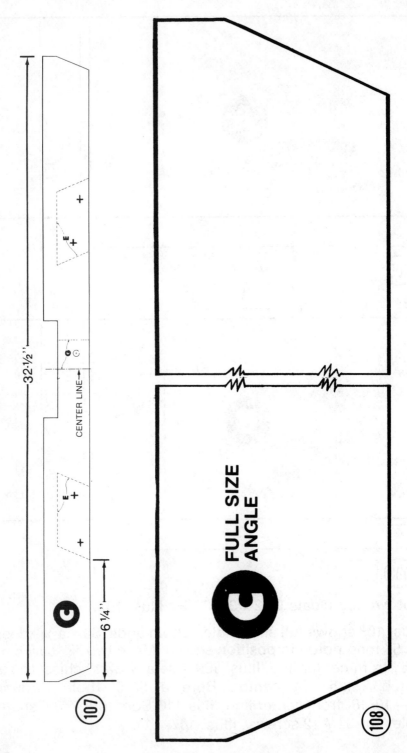

32-1/2"

6 1/4"

E

E

CENTER LINE

G

107

FULL SIZE
ANGLE

G

108

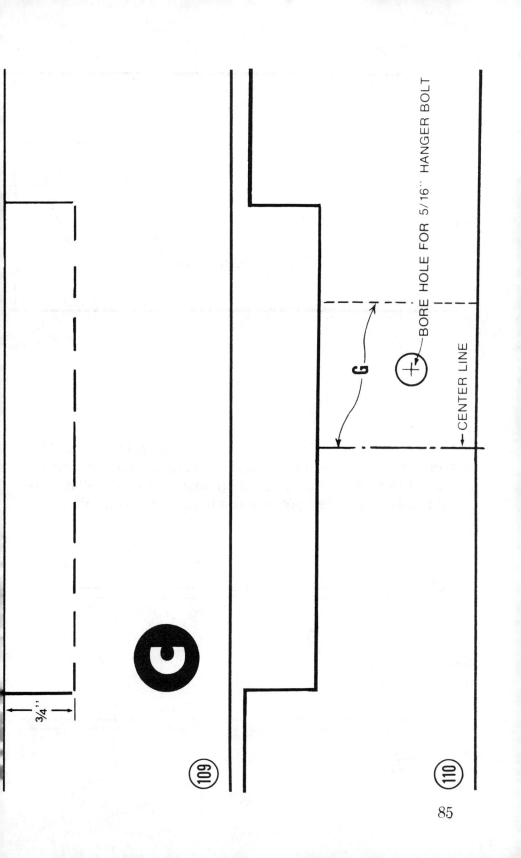

BORE HOLE FOR 5/16'' HANGER BOLT

CENTER LINE

G

C

3/4''

109

110

85

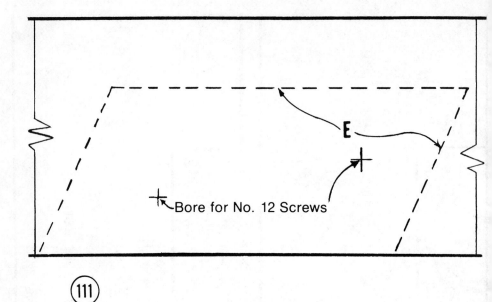

Bore for No. 12 Screws

E

⑪

Cut two leg braces D from 1 x 6 x 28⅛", Illus. 112. Bore 3/16" shank holes in position indicated, Illus. 113, for #10 screws. Illus. 114 shows position of G against D. Bore 5/16" hanger bolt hole in D when you are ready to fasten G in place.

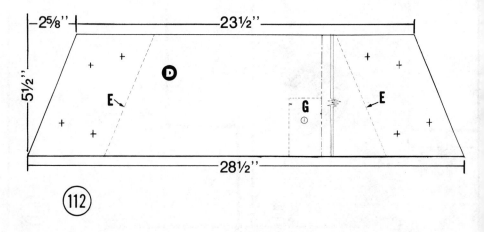

⑫

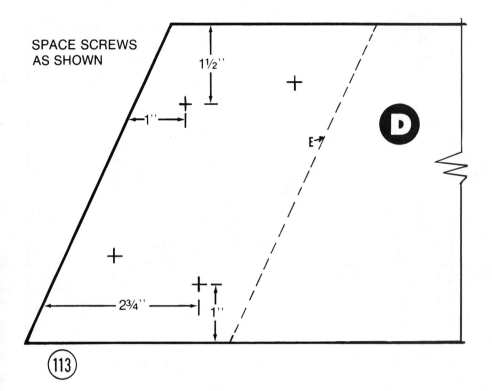

SPACE SCREWS
AS SHOWN

1½"

1"

2¾"

1"

E→

D

(113)

Cut four legs E, 2 x 4 x 32⅜", Illus. 115. Cut ends to angle shown full size, Illus. 116.

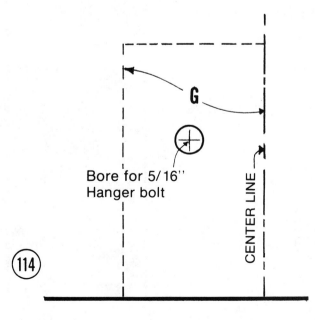

G

Bore for 5/16"
Hanger bolt

CENTER LINE

(114)

87

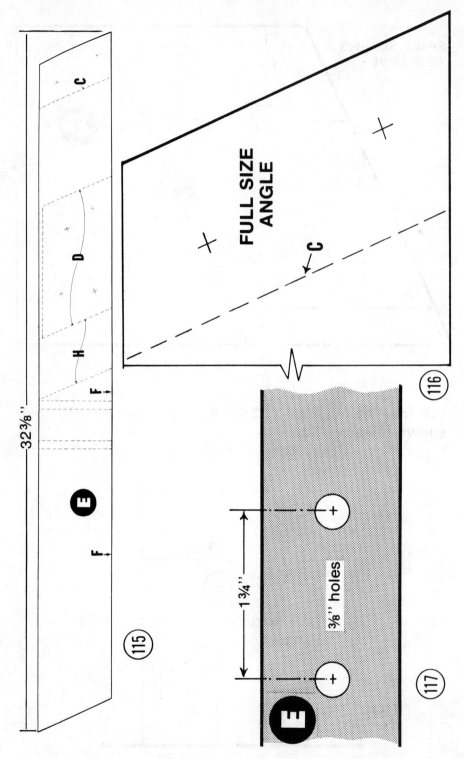

32 3/8"

E

F

F

D

H

C

115

FULL SIZE
ANGLE

C

116

3/8" holes

1 3/4"

E

117

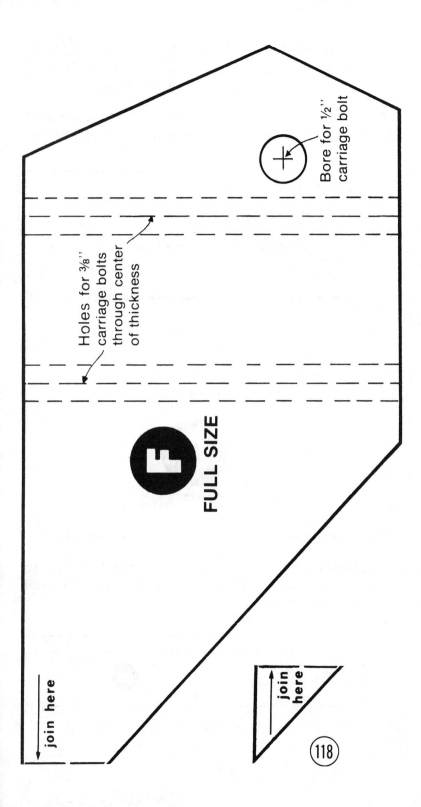

Bore for ½"
carriage bolt

Holes for ⅜"
carriage bolts
through center
of thickness

FULL SIZE

join here

join
here

(118)

Cut four seat brackets F from 2 x 6 to full size shown, Illus. 118. Bore ½" hole through F in position indicated. Do not bore the two ⅜" holes through edge at this time.

Cut two cross braces G, 2 x 3 x 49⅛", Illus. 119. Note full size angle pattern, Illus. 120. Do not bore holes through G at this time.

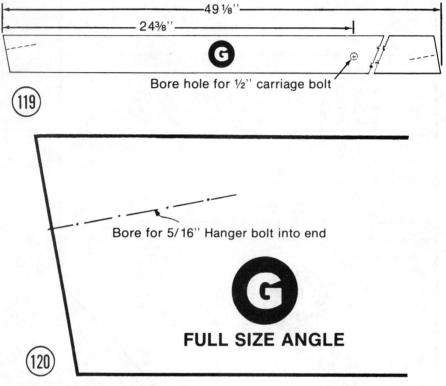

49 ⅛"

24⅜"

G

Bore hole for ½" carriage bolt

(119)

Bore for 5/16" Hanger bolt into end

G

FULL SIZE ANGLE

(120)

Cut four seat outriggers H, 2 x 3 x 20", Illus. 121. Cut ends to angle shown, Illus. 122. Do not bore ½" hole, Illus. 123, until you are ready to assemble.

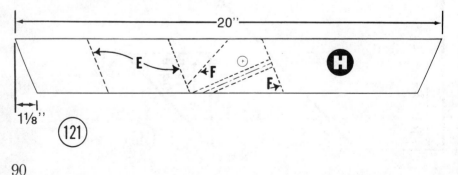

20"

E

F

H

E

1⅛"

(121)

90

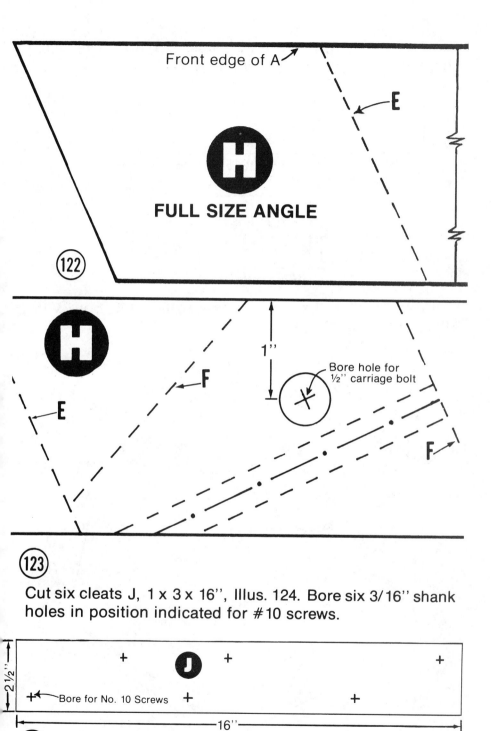

Front edge of A

E

H

FULL SIZE ANGLE

(122)

H

F

E

1"

Bore hole for
½" carriage bolt

F

(123)

Cut six cleats J, 1 x 3 x 16", Illus. 124. Bore six 3/16" shank holes in position indicated for #10 screws.

2½"

J

Bore for No. 10 Screws

16"

(124)

Cut four cleats K, 1 x 3 x 13½'', Illus. 125. Bore five 3/16''
shank holes in position shown for #10 screws.

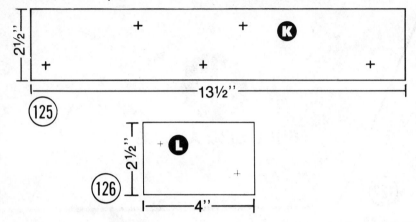

Cut four cleats L, 1 x 3, to size shown, Illus. 126. Bore 3/16''
shank holes for #10 screws.

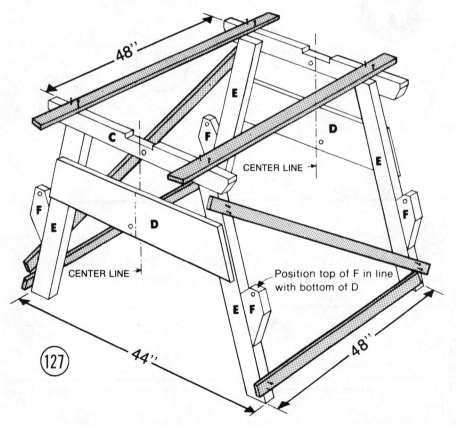

Apply waterproof glue and fasten C to E with 3" #12 screws, Illus. 107, 111, 127. Maintain position of 5/16" hole through C to left and to right of center line, Illus. 127, when assembling E to C. Legs should measure 44" across bottom. Apply glue and fasten D to E with 1¾" #10 screw.

Tack F in position, Illus. 127. Top edge of F must be level and in line with bottom edge of D. Drill ⅜" holes through F and E at angle and position shown, Illus. 118, 134. Bolt F to E with ⅜ x 8" carriage bolts.

Brace legs in position, Illus. 127. Be sure to maintain overall dimensions indicated. Tack G temporarily in position, Illus. 128. Bore through C and D into ends of G to receive a 5/16 x 4" hanger bolt, Illus. 129. If hanger bolts aren't readily available, use a 5/16 x 3½" lag screw, Illus. 130.

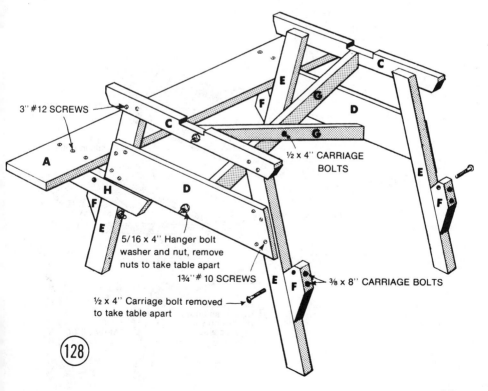

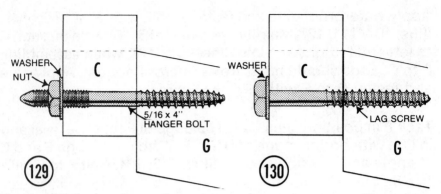

WASHER
NUT
C
5/16 x 4''
HANGER BOLT
G

(129)

WASHER
C
LAG SCREW
G

(130)

Bore ½'' hole through center where G cross, Illus. 128. Fasten with a ½ x 4'' carriage bolt.

Apply glue and screw A to H with 3'' #12 screws, Illus. 131. End of H is positioned 2½'' from edge of A. Tack AH in place. Check to make certain A and H are level. H butts against D. Insert ½'' drill through ½'' hole in F and drill through H. Fasten H to F with ¼ x 4'' carriage bolt, Illus. 128.

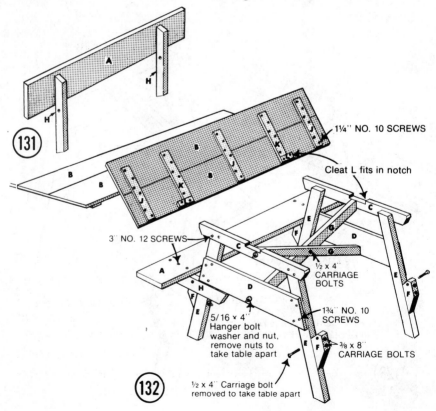

1¼'' NO. 10 SCREWS

Cleat L fits in notch

3'' NO. 12 SCREWS

½ x 4''
CARRIAGE
BOLTS

1¾'' NO. 10
SCREWS

5/16 x 4''
Hanger bolt
washer and nut,
remove nuts to
take table apart

⅜ x 8''
CARRIAGE BOLTS

(132)

½ x 4'' Carriage bolt
removed to take table apart

Apply glue and fasten cleats J, L and K in position to B with 1½" #10 screws, Illus. 132, 106. Assemble two halves as shown. Position L so it fits notch in C. This permits laying one half of top over other half when not in use.

Those making tables for public use and those who entertain overweight guests should add safety legs, Illus. 133. Hinge a leg, 2 x 4 x 16½" or length required, in position shown using 3½ x 3½" fast pin hinges.

Countersink screws. Fill holes with wood filler. Sandpaper surface before applying a wood preservative. Apply finish desired.

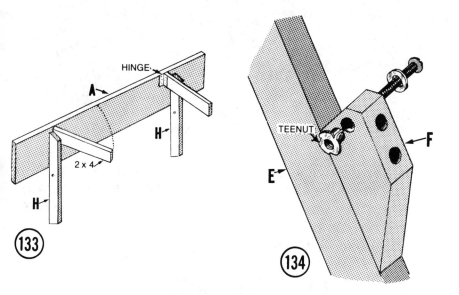

NOTE: As shown in Illus. 134, ⅜" Teenuts with ⅜" - 16 x 3½" round head stove bolts or ⅜" - 16 machine screws and washers can be used in place of the five ½ x 4" bolts specified in the list of materials. Drill ⅜" holes in F and H in place of ½" holes. To accommodate barrel of Teenut, redrill holes depth of barrel with ½" bit. Drive Teenut in position with hammer. Bolt parts together following general directions. Always keep the Teenut on inside face of F.

LAWN GLIDER

This modernized version of the old fashioned lawn glider, Illus. 135, provides almost instant relaxation. Its gentle sway soothes ruffled nerves with almost hypnotic results. Before cutting any lumber, read directions through and note location of each part shown in Illus. 138.

CUTTING DIAGRAM

1		5		6
1		5		6
1		5		6
1		5		6

5/4 x 12" x 16 FT.

7	7	7	9	9	9
7	7	7	9	9	9
14	14	14	14	12 12 12 12	

1 x 12" x 14 FT.

The frame, #1,5 and 6, should be cut from 5/4" stock. This usually runs 1 1/16 to 1⅛" thick. If you have access to a table saw, 5/4 x 12" x 16' can provide parts #1, 5, 6, Illus. 136. One 1 x 12" x 14' can provide parts #7, 9, 12 and 14. If 5/4 x 12" x 16' is hard to come by, use one 5/4 x 12" x 8', two 5/4 x 6" x 8' for #5 and 6. To simplifiy positioning parts and drilling holes where needed, parts of full size patterns are shown in Illus. 139, 140, 141, 142, 143, 144, 145, 146, 147, 149, 150, 152, 153, 154, 155, 158, 159, 160, 163, 164, 165, 167, 168, 169, 172. To double check, drill holes after placing parts in position.

⊙ indicates where to drill shank hole for screw. + indicates part receiving point of screw. Countersink shank holes.

Illus. 137 indicates overall size of each part. Cut each to exact size indicated. Sandpaper each part.

LIST OF MATERIALS

1 — 5/4 x 12 x 16' - #1,5,6 Illus. 137, 138.
1 — 1 x 6 x 12' - #2,3
8 — 1 x 4 x 10' - #4,8,15,17
1 — 1 x 12 x 14' - #7,9,12,14
2 — 1 x 4 x 14' - #10
1 — 1 x 6 x 14' - #11
1 — 1 x 6 x 10' - #13,16
2 — 7/16 x 46" iron rod threaded on ends, nuts - #19
2 — 7/16 x 52"   "   "   "   "   "
4 — ⅜ x 3" - A,galvanized or black threaded pipe nipples and nuts
4 — ⅜ x 2" - B   "   "   "   "   "   "
10 — ⅜ x 1½" - C   "   "   "   "   "   "
6 — 5/16 x 2¼" - D,carriage bolts, nuts and washers
12 — 5/16 x 2¾" - E   "   "   "   "
2 — 5/16 x 1½" - F   "   "   "   "
36 lock nuts to fit threaded nipple
16 — 2" #12 flathead screws
17 doz. 1¾" #10 flathead screws
Waterproof glue

⅜" nipples and lock nuts can be obtained in electrical supply stores. Actual inside dimension is 7/16". Or ½ x 1½" nipples and nuts can be used. In this case, drill holes to fit nipple.

PART NO.	ITEM & REMARKS	NO. PCS.	FINISHED DIMENSIONS	WOOD
1	Frame	4	1⅛" x 2¾" x 7'10"	W. Pine
2	Frame, Bottom Rail	2	¾" x 2¾" x 6'2⅜"	,,
3	,, Top Rail	2	¾" x 2¾" x 4'1¾"	,,
4	,, Cap	2	¾" x 3½" x 4'¾"	,,
5	,, Brace	4	1⅛" x 2¾" x 2'2"	,,
6	,, Diag. Brace	4	1⅛" x 2¾" x 5'4¾"	,,
7	Back, Sides	6	¾" x 4" x 2'9"	,,
8	,, Slats	24	¾" x 1¾" x 3'3"	,,
9	Seat, Sides	6	¾" x 4¾" x 1'8¼"	,,
10	,, Slats	16	¾" x 1¾" x 3'4½"	,,
11	Hanger	4	¾" x 2¼" x 7'	,,
12	Spacer, 2" Round	4	¾" x 2" x 2"	,,
13	Tie	4	¾" x 2¼" x 1'3¾"	,,
14	Arms	4	¾" x 3" x 1'11"	,,
15	Tie Rails	2	¾" x 1¾" x 3'8"	,,
16	Floor, Rails	3	¾" x 2¼" x 3'10¾"	,,
17	Floor Slats	15	¾" x 1¾" x 3'3"	,,
18	,, Diagonal Brace	2	¾" x 1½" x Length Required	,,

(137)

Illus. 138 indicates position of parts #1 through #19, also location of each nipple and carriage bolt. These are keyed as follows: A — ⅜ x 3'' nipple; B — ⅜ x 2''; C — ⅜ x 1½''; D — 5/16 x 2½'' carriage bolt; E — 5/16 x 2¾''; F — 5/16 x 1½''.

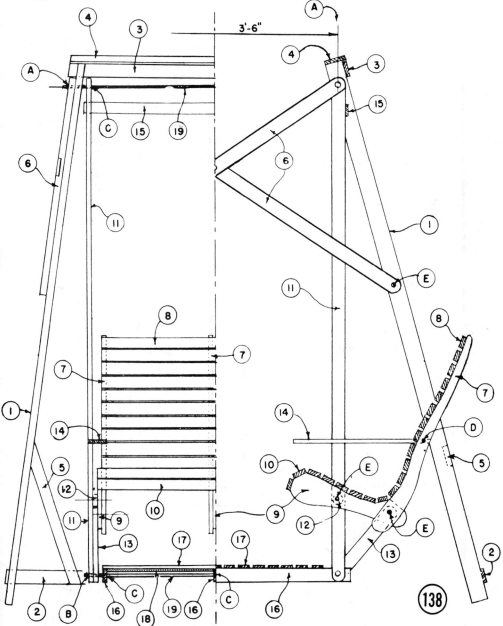

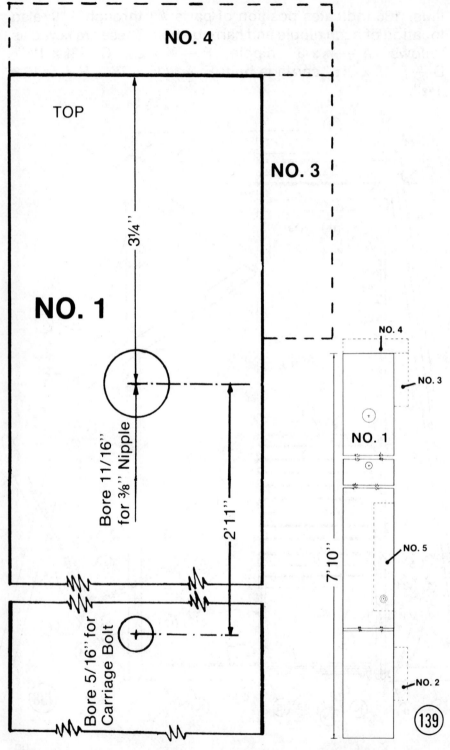

TOP

NO. 4

NO. 3

NO. 1

3¼"

Bore 11/16"
for ⅜" Nipple

2'11"

Bore 5/16" for
Carriage Bolt

NO. 4

NO. 3

NO. 1

NO. 5

NO. 2

7'10"

139

100

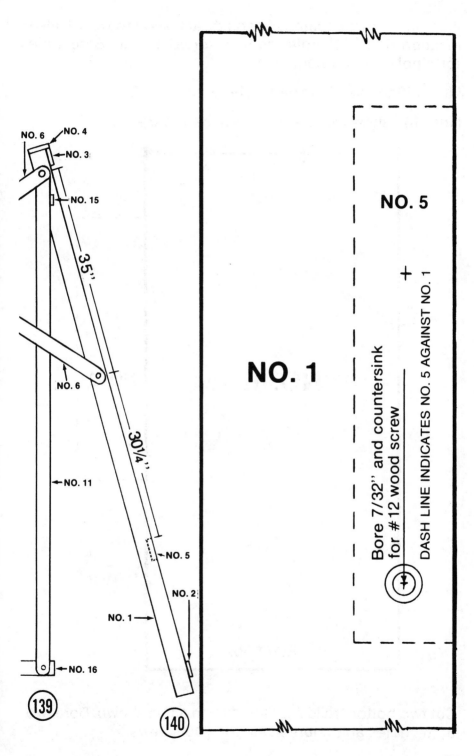

NO. 6
NO. 4
NO. 3
NO. 15

35"

NO. 6

30¼"

NO. 11

NO. 5

NO. 2

NO. 1

NO. 16

(139)

(140)

NO. 5

+

Bore 7/32" and countersink for #12 wood screw

DASH LINE INDICATES NO. 5 AGAINST NO. 1

NO. 1

Illus. 139 shows position of parts #3 and #4 at top of #1; also location of 11/16'' hole required for ⅜'' nipple. Bore hole for nipple and carriage bolt.

Illus. 140 shows where part #5 butts against #1.

Illus. 141 shows where #2 is fastened to #1.

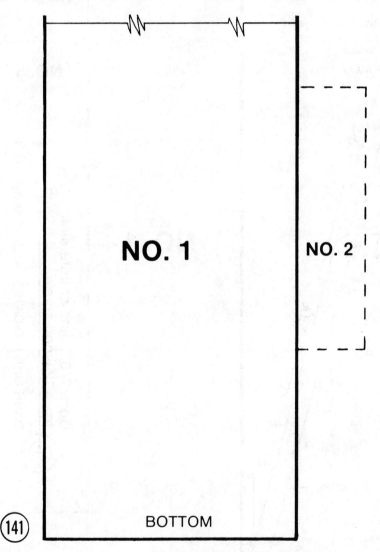

NO. 1

NO. 2

(141)

BOTTOM

Cut two bottom rails #2, Illus. 142, to angle shown. Bore two 3/16'' holes and countersink for #10 screws.

Illus. 143 shows #5 finishing flush with bottom of #2. Drill shank holes for #10 screws in #2 after placing #5 in position.

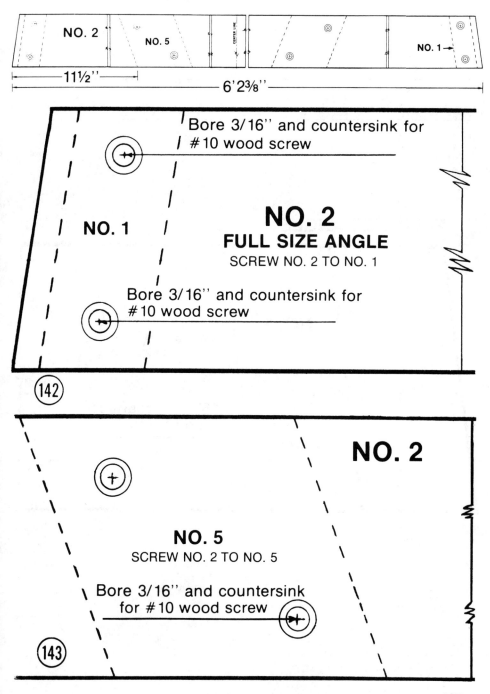

11½"

6'2⅜"

NO. 2

NO. 5

NO. 1→

Bore 3/16" and countersink for #10 wood screw

NO. 1

NO. 2
FULL SIZE ANGLE
SCREW NO. 2 TO NO. 1

Bore 3/16" and countersink for #10 wood screw

(142)

NO. 2

NO. 5
SCREW NO. 2 TO NO. 5

Bore 3/16" and countersink for #10 wood screw

(143)

Cut two top rails #3 to size specified and to angle shown full size, Illus. 144. Note position of part #1.

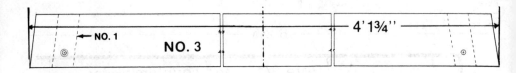

FULL SIZE ANGLE

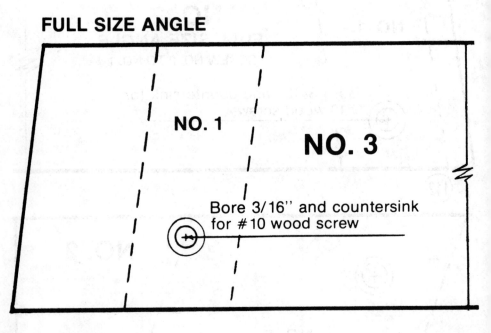

NO. 1

NO. 3

Bore 3/16'' and countersink for #10 wood screw

(144)

Cut two caps #4, Illus. 145. Note position of 3/16" holes for #12 and #10 screws.

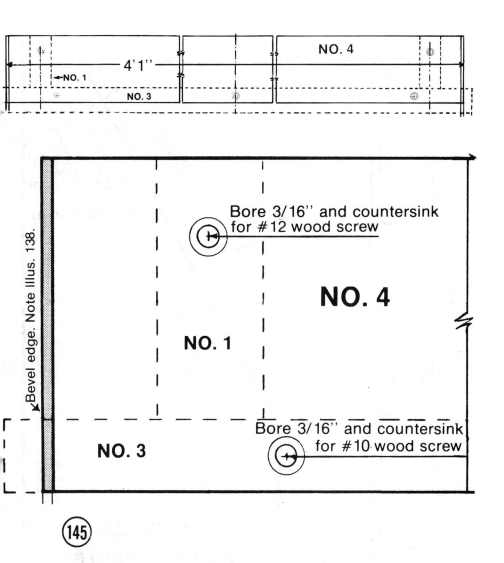

Bevel edge. Note Illus. 138.

4'1"

NO. 1

NO. 3

NO. 4

Bore 3/16" and countersink for #12 wood screw

NO. 4

NO. 1

NO. 3

Bore 3/16" and countersink for #10 wood screw

(145)

Cut four braces #5. Illus. 146 shows angle required where #5 butts against #1. Bore a 7/32" shank hole through edge of #5. This permits fastening #5 to #1.

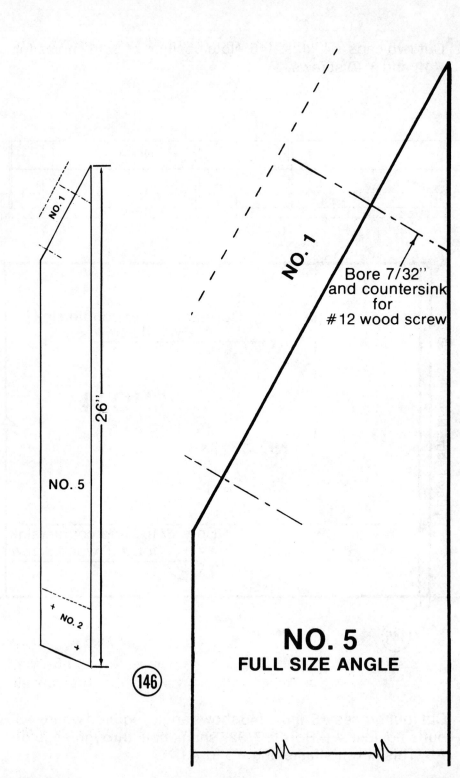

NO. 1

Bore 7/32"
and countersink
for
#12 wood screw

2'6"

NO. 5

NO. 1

NO. 2

(146)

NO. 5
FULL SIZE ANGLE

106

Illus. 147 shows angle required where #2 is fastened to #5. Note Illus. 138.

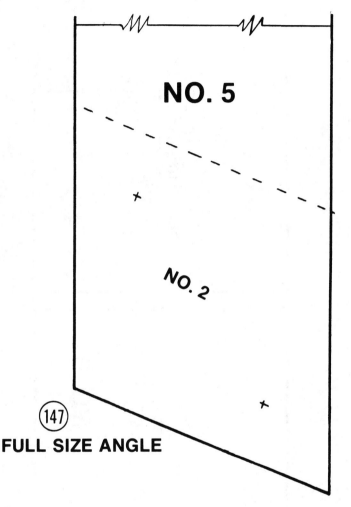

NO. 5

NO. 2

147
FULL SIZE ANGLE

Apply glue and fasten #2, 3 and 4 to #1, Illus. 138. Drive one screw through #1 into #5, the other through #5 into #1. Fasten #2 to #5, #4 to #3 with #10 screws. Countersink all screws.

Cut four #6, Illus. 148. Illus. 149 shows full size shape of ends, also location of 11/16 and 5/16" holes.

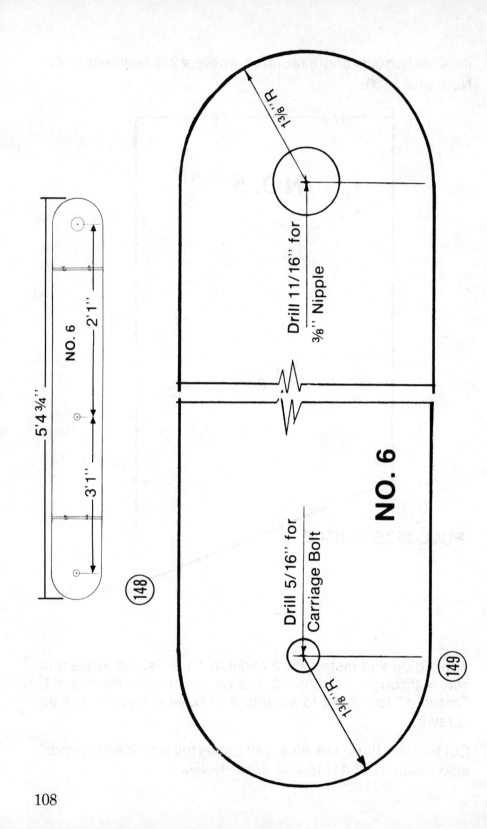

NO. 6

5' 4 3/4"

2' 1"

3' 1"

148

Drill 11/16" for
3/8" Nipple

1 3/8" R

NO. 6

Drill 5/16" for
Carriage Bolt

1 3/8" R

149

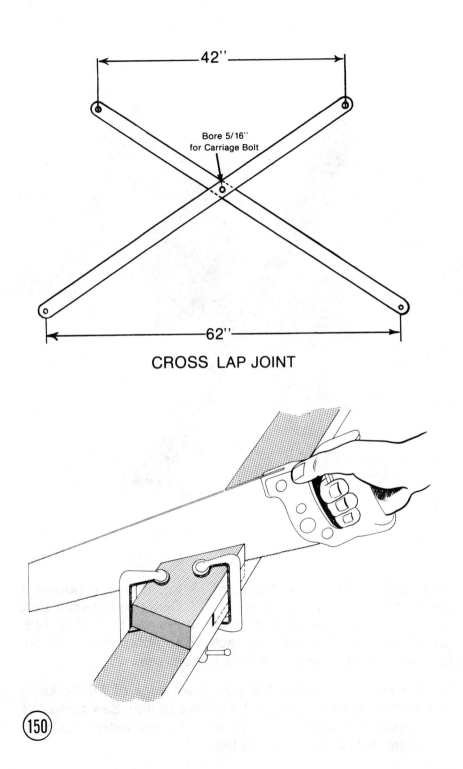

42"

Bore 5/16"
for Carriage Bolt

62"

CROSS LAP JOINT

150

109

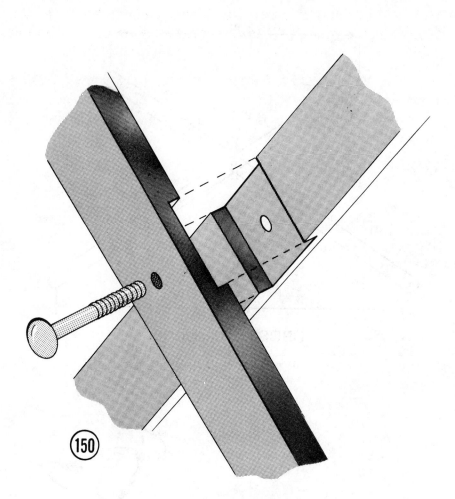

(150)

Illus. 150 shows cross lap joint in #6. Distance between nipple holes, center to center is 42". Distance between bolt holes 62". Mark center of hole for nipple and bolt, Illus. 149, but do not drill. Temporarily tack #6 together and drill hole for center bolt. Draw lines where #6 cross.

Draw lines for cross lap halfway down edge of #6. To keep saw plumb, clamp a piece of 1 x 2 along line. Saw to half of thickness. Place edge up in a vise and chisel mortise using a 1" chisel. Finish joint with a file.

Bolt #6 together at cross lap. Clamp assembled #6 to #1, Illus. 138. Maintain 42" spread across top. Insert bit through #1 and drill hole for nipple in #6, also for bolt.

Insert ⅜ x 3" nipple at A. Fasten #6 and #1 with lock nuts on nipple. Bolt #6 to #1 at E with 5/16 x 2¾" carriage bolts.

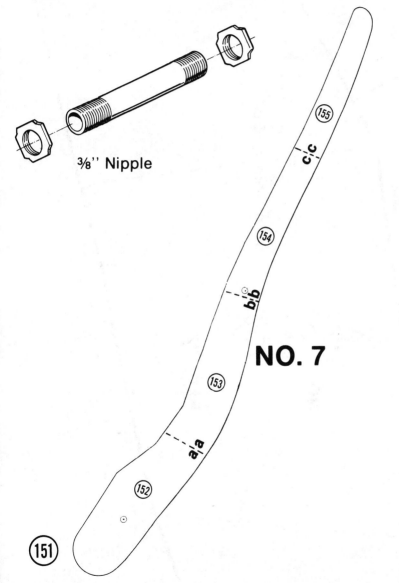

⅜" Nipple

NO. 7

The seat back #7, Illus. 151, is shown full size in Illus. 152, 153, 154, 155. Draw a full size pattern and cut six #7.

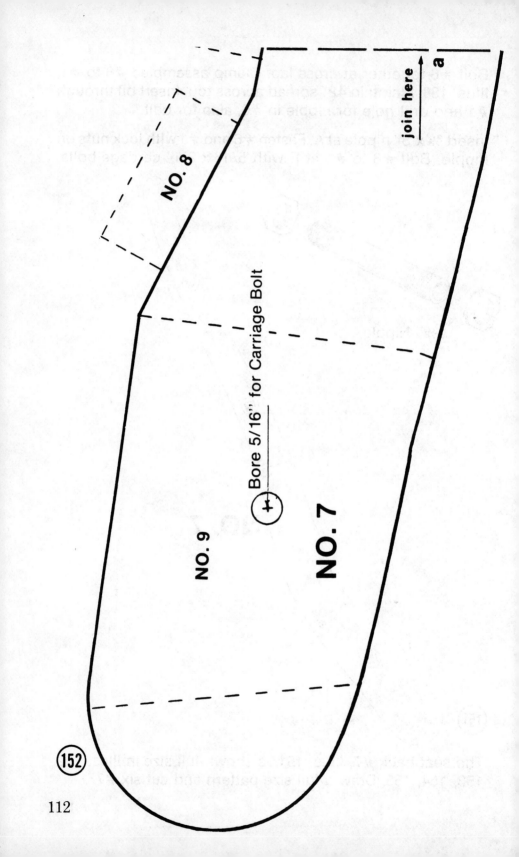

NO. 8

NO. 9

NO. 7

join here

a

Bore 5/16" for Carriage Bolt

(152)

112

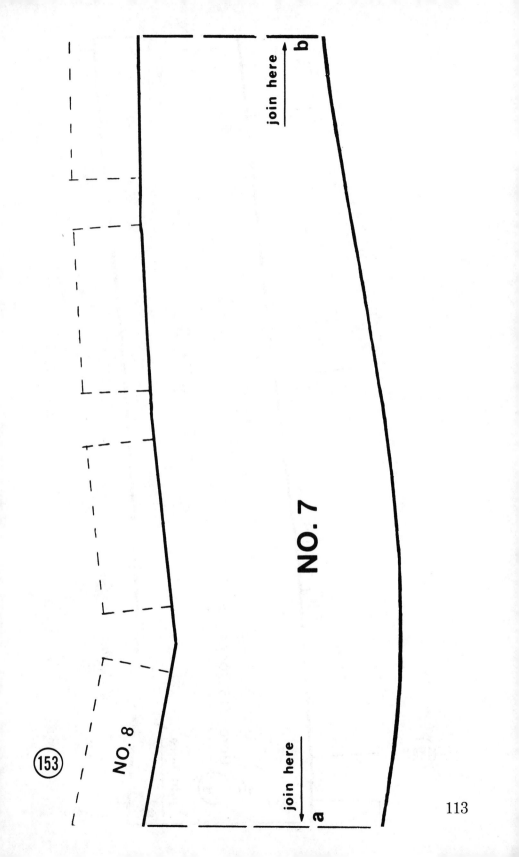

NO. 7

NO. 8

join here a

join here b

(153)

113

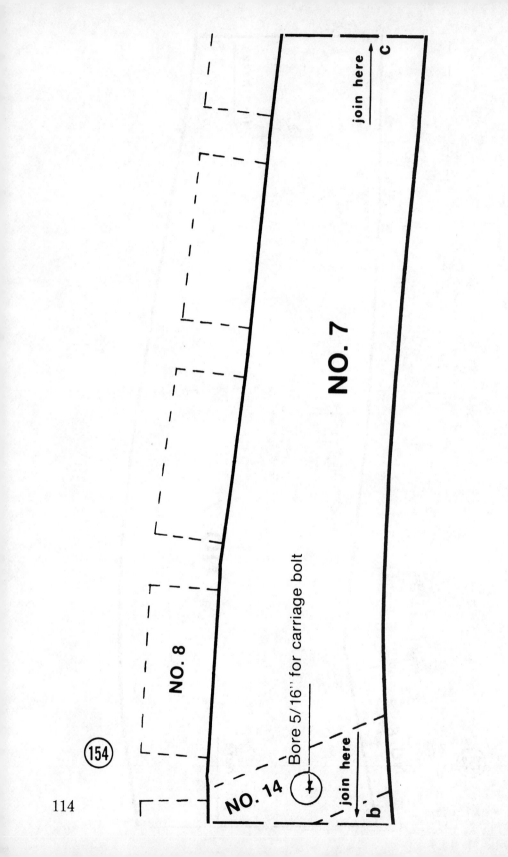

NO. 7

NO. 8

NO. 14

join here

c

join here

b

Bore 5/16" for carriage bolt

(154)

114

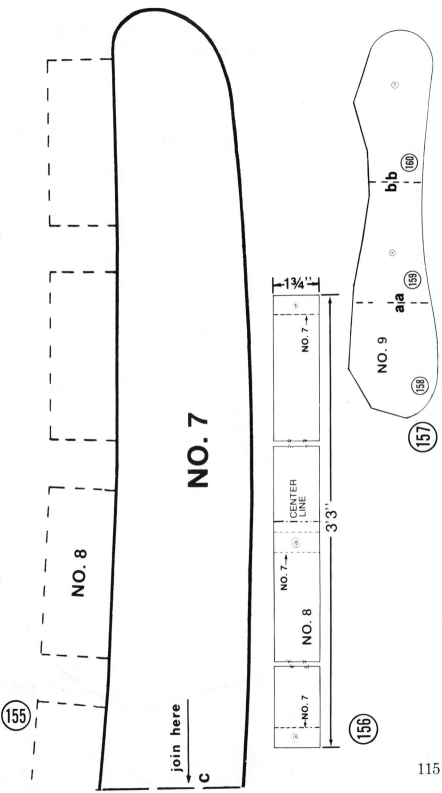

NO. 7

NO. 8

join here
c

⑮155

─1¾"─

NO. 7

CENTER
LINE

NO. 7

NO. 8

NO. 7

3'3"

⑯156

NO. 9

b┊b

⑯160

⑯159

a┊a

⑯158

⑯157

115

Cut twenty-four back rest slats #8, Illus. 156. Drill 3/16'' holes in position shown. Round top edge, Illus. 161.

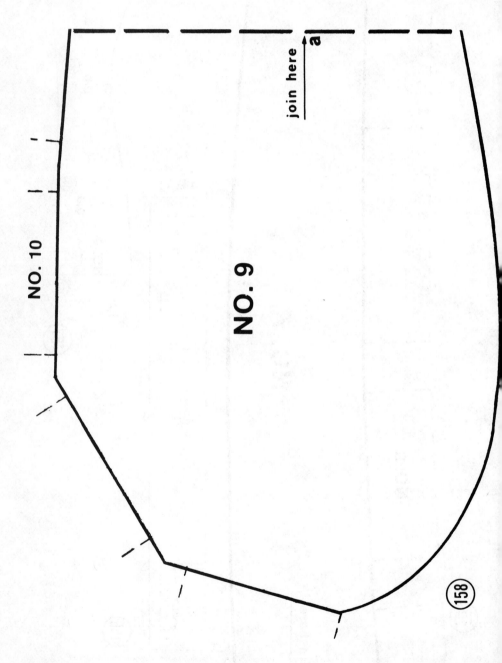

join here

a

NO. 10

NO. 9

(158)

Trace Illus. 158, 159, 160 to draw up a full size pattern for #9, Illus. 157. Cut six.

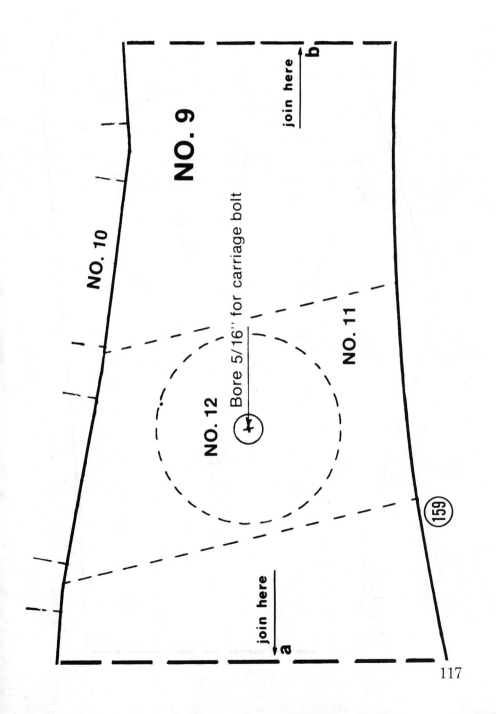

117

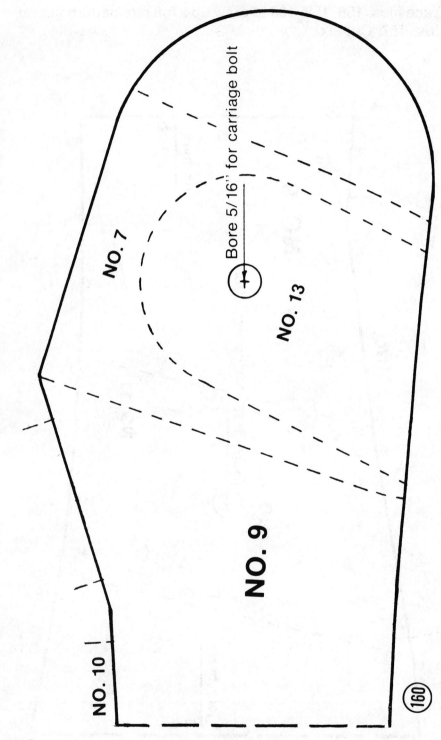

Bore 5/16" for carriage bolt

NO. 7

NO. 13

NO. 9

NO. 10

160

118

Cut sixteen seat slats #10, Illus. 161. Drill 3/16" holes in position noted. Apply glue and fasten #10 to #9 and #8 to #7 in position indicated.

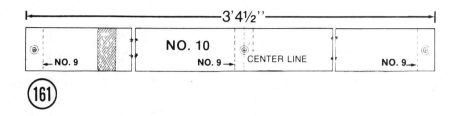

Cut four hangers #11, Illus. 162. Drill 11/16" hole 1⅛" from bottom, Illus. 163, and 1½" from top.

Cut four 2" round spacers from ¾" stock, Illus. 164.

Cut four seat supports #13, Illus. 165.

Clamp #13 in position to bottom of #11 and bore 11/16" hole to receive ⅜ x 2" nipple. Insert nipple. Fasten #11 to #13 with lock nuts.

Bolt #13, #9, #7 together at E, Illus. 138, 160, with a 5/16 x 2¾" carriage bolt.

Insert #12 between #11 and #9 and fasten with a 5/16 x 2¾" carriage bolt, Illus. 159.

Bolt middle #9 and #7 together using 5/16 x 2¼" carriage bolt.

Draw a full size pattern for arm #14, Illus. 166, from Illus. 167, 168, 169. Cut four #14. Cut notch to size hanger #11 requires. Drill 5/16" hole through center of #14 in position shown, Illus. 167. Bolt #14 to #7 at D using 5/16 x 2¼" carriage bolt, Illus. 138. Fasten #11 to #14 with 2" #12 flathead screw, Illus. 168, 169.

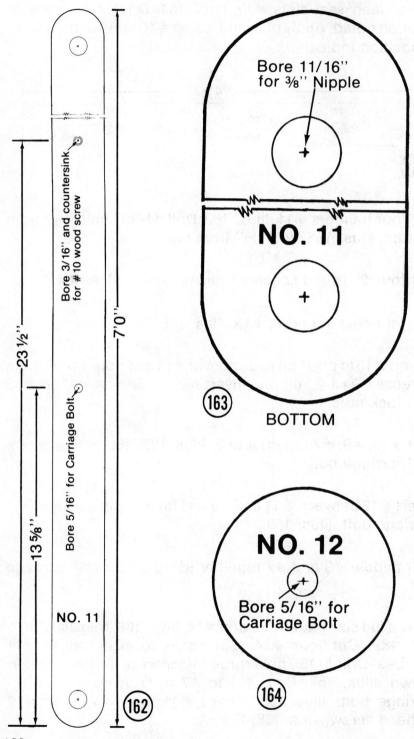

Bore 11/16'' for 3/8'' Nipple

NO. 11

163

BOTTOM

NO. 12

Bore 5/16'' for Carriage Bolt

164

23 1/2''

7'0''

13 5/8''

Bore 3/16'' and countersink for #10 wood screw

Bore 5/16'' for Carriage Bolt

NO. 11

162

120

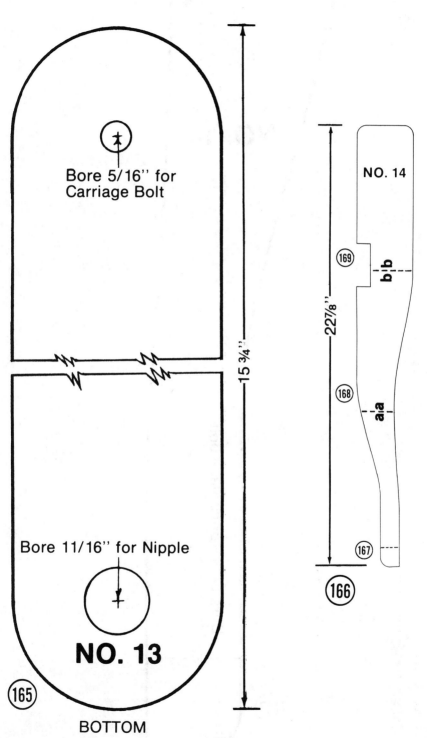

Bore 5/16'' for
Carriage Bolt

Bore 11/16'' for Nipple

NO. 13

15 3/4''

NO. 14

22⁷/₈''

b b

a a

169

168

167

166

165

BOTTOM

121

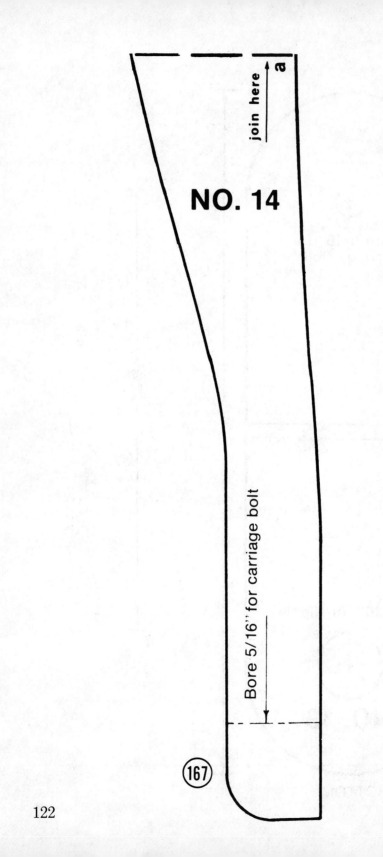

NO. 14

join here

a

Bore 5/16" for carriage bolt

(167)

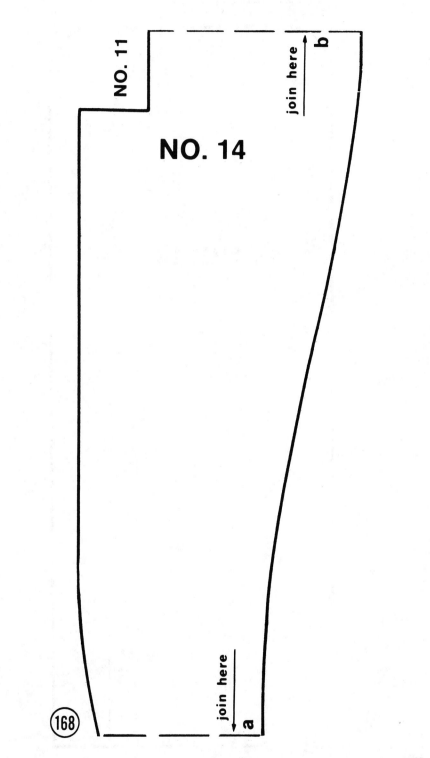

NO. 11

NO. 14

join here
b

join here
a

168

123

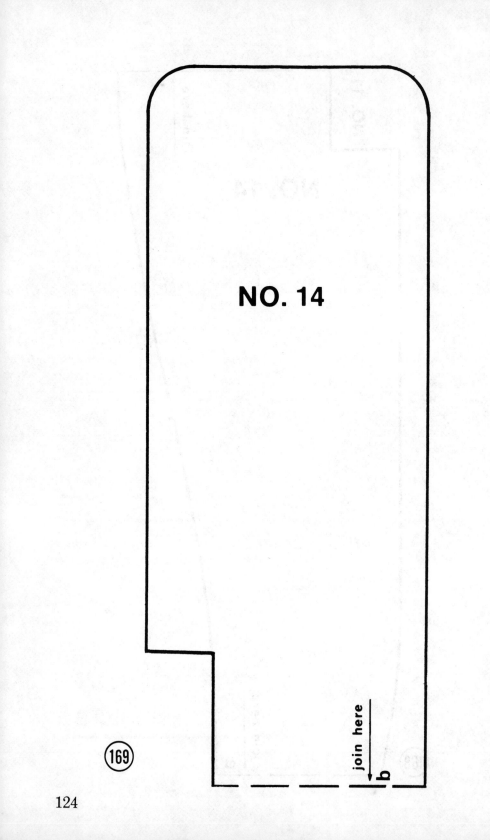

NO. 14

join here

b

Cut two tie rails #15, Illus. 170. Bore 3/16" holes in position indicated. Fasten #15 to #11 with 1¾" #10 screws 5" down from top of #11, Illus. 138.

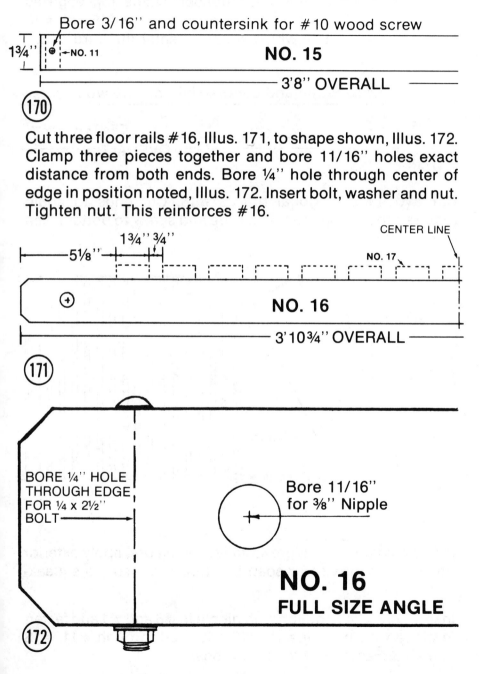

Bore 3/16" and countersink for #10 wood screw

1¾" ⊕ ←NO. 11

NO. 15

3'8" OVERALL

⑰⓪

Cut three floor rails #16, Illus. 171, to shape shown, Illus. 172. Clamp three pieces together and bore 11/16" holes exact distance from both ends. Bore ¼" hole through center of edge in position noted, Illus. 172. Insert bolt, washer and nut. Tighten nut. This reinforces #16.

CENTER LINE

5⅛"   1¾" ¾"

NO. 17

NO. 16

3'10¾" OVERALL

⑰①

BORE ¼" HOLE THROUGH EDGE FOR ¼ x 2½" BOLT

Bore 11/16" for ⅜" Nipple

NO. 16
FULL SIZE ANGLE

⑰②

Insert ⅜ x 1½'' nipple. Fasten in position with lock nuts.

Cut fifteen floor slats #17, Illus. 173. Drill 3/16'' holes where indicated. Using a file or sandpaper, shape top edge as shown, Illus. 18. Apply glue and fasten #17 to #16 with #10 screws. Check frame with a square. Center the third #16.

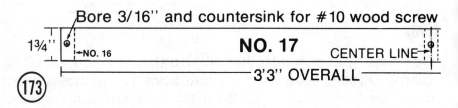

Bore 3/16'' and countersink for #10 wood screw

1¾'' NO. 16   NO. 17   CENTER LINE

3'3'' OVERALL

(173)

Cut two 1 x 2 diagonal braces #18. Cut ends to angle required to butt against #16. Glue and screw to bottom face of #17, Illus. 174.

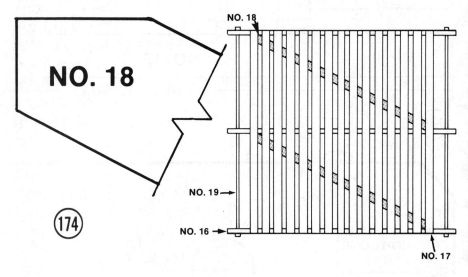

NO. 18

NO. 18

NO. 19→

NO. 16 →

(174)

NO. 17

Apply a coat of wood preservative. When dry, apply exterior paint. Apply grease or soap to nipples to insure a squeak-proof ride.

Insert 7/16 x 52'' rod through nipple in #6 and #1 and fasten in place with nuts. Insert 7/16 x 46'' rod through #11, #13 and #16. Fasten nut to end of rods.

To Earn a Living Without Pressure

Solving a problem, and particularly those that determine how well or long we may live, is no small accomplishment. As many pundits have frequently stated, adversity is one of life's best teachers.

I learned this fact of life during the ten year Depression of the thirties. Jobs were scarce but I managed to go from one to another. Since I was willing, enthusiastic and hungry, I accepted any job available at whatever salary was offered. This necessitated living on a tight budget. When my bride wanted to buy six window valances which I felt we couldn't afford, I decided to "make them myself." Not being too skillful, and not wishing to waste lumber, then selling at 4½¢ a foot, I drew up a full size pattern on wrapping paper. When this was redrawn the needed number of times to finally meet my wife's approval, I traced the outline on lumber. Using a 25¢ coping saw, I cut and assembled six for what one would have cost purchased readymade.

In the following months, I used the same procedure to build a bookcase, corner cupboard and other projects. The pattern served two important functions; it helped eliminate fear of wasting lumber, and secondly, it insured results. As friends and neighbors began to borrow the patterns and achieved equal results, I decided to start Easi-Bild full size woodworking patterns — a first in 1938. The patterns and, much later, Easi-Bild home repair and improvement books grew into a profitable corporation with world wide sales.

All through life, we strive to find our niche. One that provides both a living and an acceptable way of life. To hold a job, all too many allow their peers to influence daily decisions. Many live under far too much tension and use alcohol or drugs to find relief. Focusing one's mentalens — your mind's eye — on a new sphere of activity, doing today something you didn't think you could do yesterday, provides relief from tension, rebuilds one's ego and self confidence. It's life's way of creating an individual.

Learning to build what others want and can afford to buy provides constructive escape. It enables those who need it the most to create a new way of life without gambling their savings.

Time is your most precious inheritance. How you use, waste or invest it dictates how you will live. The time paid for by others helps earn a living while one's spare time offers great investment opportunities. Your mind is the world's best computer and can be programmed to materialize your fondest dreams, generate peace of mind, maintain good health and greatly extend one's lifespan. Just as this book takes the fear, mystery and far more than half the cost out of building outdoor furniture, others in this series can help you build a one, two or three bedroom house. You, the operator of the world's best computer, must be willing to TRY.

Among the most popular of my early patterns were those that simplified construction of outdoor furniture. Almost every-one who saw and sat in the chairs illustrated wanted duplicates. Because of today's excessive trucking rates, you can build and sell them localy at a profit. Letters from almost every state and places as distant as Guam, Samoa, Nova Scotia to New Zealand tell how building these pieces for their own use helped them start a part or full time business.

As this book goes to press, the nation faces a huge unem-ployment and costly housing problem that affects the lives of at least one member of every family. Millions of others face a forced sale or foreclosure of their homes. The solution to finding work, or saving a home, rests solely with what you do. Begin today. The opportunities are unlimited.

Consider how massive recalls and high cost have destroyed

public confidence in the auto industry; how OPEC pricing conditioned users to conserve gas and heating oil. Consider how the building industry has priced housing out of reach of the intelligent buyer. These basic economic facts create great potential for everyone, those unemployed, retirees to youth about to enter the labor force.

A huge percentage of all homes are owned by retirees and those approaching retirement. Most use far less space than they previously needed. Converting a basement, attic, garage or building an addition with an outside entry, enables every owner to obtain rental income from the more than 13,000,000 singles and couples currently searching for a place they can afford.

Easi-Bild Books explain how to do this work in words and pictures everyone can follow. Creating an apartment offers on site job experience for every member of the family. Those who convert or build rental space soon discover they can do the same work for as many others as they can handle.

Creating an apartment that can generate instant monthly income, building and displaying lawn furniture where passersby can see, inspect and price, doesn't require sales experience. People buy far more of what they want than anyone sells. This fact is confirmed by letters from those who have already experienced results. Depending on the season of the year, they build toys or workbenches with equal enthusiasm.

One facet described in many letters concerned their inability to get started. Being laid off with little or no hope of re-employment after years on the job stunned many. This surfaced in letters from auto workers. As computerized robots took over an assembly line, thousands were jolted out of jobs many had held for ten, twenty or more years. Economists readily admit these jobs will never again be done by human hands. Regardless of what type of blue or white collar job an individual presently holds, a robot could shape their lives in the months ahead. Consider how you will cope. Expect change. Insulate your thinking from being surprised. Readjusting your mind's eye on new spheres of activity should begin immediately. What has already happened to millions could happen to you.

The record high number of home foreclosures that occurred in the fourth quarter of 1982 indicates planning for one's future must start early in life. Investing an abundance of free time converting unused space into a rental apartment can save both a home from foreclosure and the mind of the owner. As a starter consider converting a garage into a one bedroom studio apartment as described in Book #684. If you don't have a garage, but do own sufficient space for one, consider building a two car garage with an apartment above as described in Book #763.

Solving problems is life's method of adding purpose, pride and self confidence. This was clearly illustrated in a letter we received many years ago from a young teacher. He was assigned to start a special study course, one in which the school had no previous experience. The school supervisor told him he had to "create procedure."

His students came from two groups of youth. One group was retarded, the second blind. Imaginative and willing to tackle any job offered, he found the most difficult part was the urgent need to establish communication. He had to make certain each student understood exactly what he wanted them to do. Having just moved into the community and lacking funds needed to furnish a home, he had sent for our lawn furniture patterns. He decided to show his first group, retardees with no previous school experience, how to build a lawn chair.

Realizing the pattern would be used over and over again, he traced each part on a 4 x 8 sheet of ⅛" hardboard. Using a coping saw, he cut each part to exact shape of the pattern. Next he drilled the exact size holes, through the template, the pattern indicated.

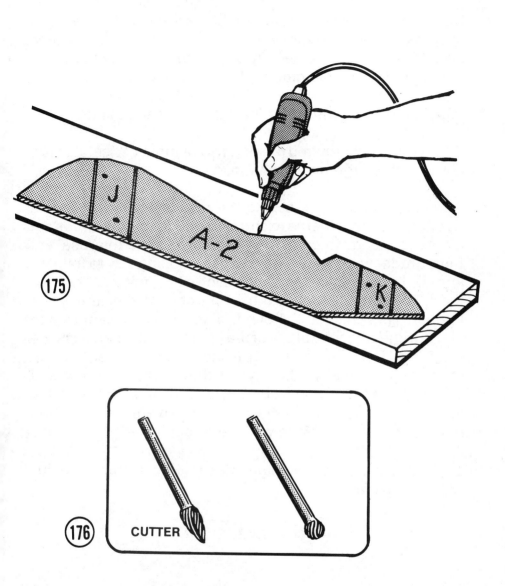

Where leg J, Illus. 34, was fastened to A, he outlined its exact position on the template. To emphasize its angle and to help the blind feel and "see" its position, he etched its position using a small electric tool and 7/32" cutter, Illus.175.

To make certain each student would remember the identity of each part, he used a 7/32" diameter ball cutter, Illus. 176, to outline the same letter used on the pattern.

He soon discovered a retardee became more familiar with each part when they ran their fingers over the routed outline even though all could see. By using the ball cutter to outline position of each adjoining part, such as J to A, H to J, K to A, Illus. 35, he developed a teaching aid that proved outstandingly successful with retardees as well as the blind.

When a project required making two or more of a single part, he routed a large two on the part.

A third grade teacher, seeing the results achieved, made a duplicate set of patterns to show her students how important it was to "learn to earn." In both classes the retardee and third grader were shown how to use a coping saw to follow a line. To help the blind feel and "see" a line, the teacher used the 7/32" cutter to outline the ⅛" hardboard template on the lumber. This enabled the blind to develop sufficient skill to feel the line while the blade of the jig saw cut the part to shape required. The letter went on to describe how each group experienced great pride in what they built when selected pieces were placed on sale at a school sponsored auction. In each case the name of the builder was mentioned over the microphone as the piece was being auctioned.

Good direction and a willingness to make a dream come true requires TRYING.

EB

HANDY - REFERENCE - LUMBER
PLYWOOD - FLAKEBOARD - HARDBOARD - MOLDINGS

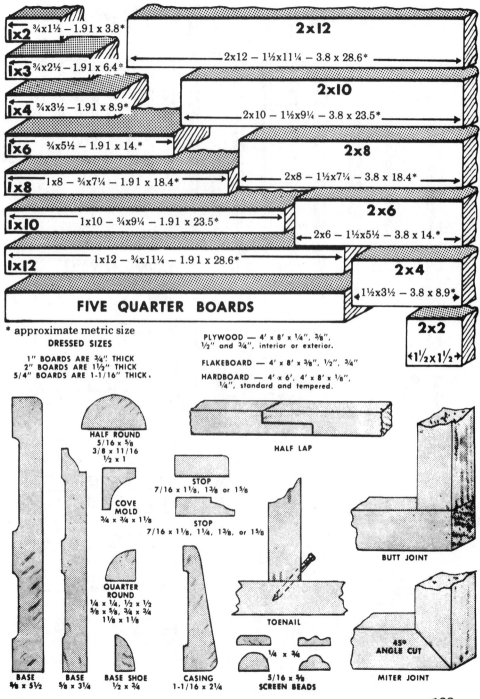

1x2 ¾x1½ — 1.91 x 3.8*

2x12

2x12 — 1½x11¼ — 3.8 x 28.6*

1x3 ¾x2½ — 1.91 x 6.4*

2x10

2x10 — 1½x9¼ — 3.8 x 23.5*

1x4 ¾x3½ — 1.91 x 8.9*

2x8

1x6 ¾x5½ — 1.91 x 14.*

2x8 — 1½x7¼ — 3.8 x 18.4*

1x8 1x8 — ¾x7¼ — 1.91 x 18.4*

2x6

1x10 1x10 — ¾x9¼ — 1.91 x 23.5*

2x6 — 1½x5½ — 3.8 x 14.*

1x12 1x12 — ¾x11¼ — 1.91 x 28.6*

2x4

1½x3½ — 3.8 x 8.9*

FIVE QUARTER BOARDS

2x2

1½x1½

* approximate metric size
DRESSED SIZES

1" BOARDS ARE ¾" THICK
2" BOARDS ARE 1½" THICK
5/4" BOARDS ARE 1-1/16" THICK.

PLYWOOD — 4' x 8' x ¼", ⅜",
½" and ¾", interior or exterior.

FLAKEBOARD — 4' x 8' x ⅜", ½", ¾"

HARDBOARD — 4' x 6', 4' x 8' x ⅛",
¼", standard and tempered.

HALF ROUND
5/16 x ⅝
3/8 x 11/16
½ x 1

HALF LAP

STOP
7/16 x 1⅛, 1⅜ or 1⅝

COVE
MOLD
¾ x ¾ x 1⅛

STOP
7/16 x 1⅛, 1¼, 1⅜, or 1⅝

BUTT JOINT

QUARTER
ROUND
¼ x ¼, ½ x ½
⅝ x ⅝, ¾ x ¾
1⅛ x 1⅛

TOENAIL

45°
ANGLE CUT

BASE
⅝ x 5½

BASE
⅝ x 3¼

BASE SHOE
½ x ¾

CASING
1-1/16 x 2¼

¼ x ¾
5/16 x ⅝
SCREEN BEADS

MITER JOINT

133

HANDY REFERENCE-NAILS Common─ Finishing─

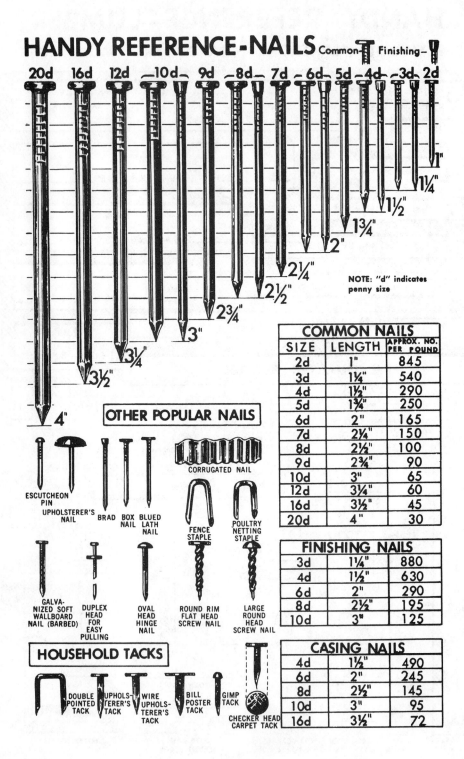

20d 16d 12d ─10d─ 9d ─8d─ 7d ─6d─ 5d ─4d─ ─3d─ 2d

1"

1¼"

1½"

1¾"

2"

2¼"

2½"

2¾"

3"

3¼"

3½"

4"

NOTE: "d" indicates penny size

OTHER POPULAR NAILS

CORRUGATED NAIL

ESCUTCHEON PIN

UPHOLSTERER'S NAIL

BRAD BOX NAIL BLUED LATH NAIL

FENCE STAPLE

POULTRY NETTING STAPLE

GALVA-NIZED SOFT WALLBOARD NAIL (BARBED)

DUPLEX HEAD FOR EASY PULLING

OVAL HEAD HINGE NAIL

ROUND RIM FLAT HEAD SCREW NAIL

LARGE ROUND HEAD SCREW NAIL

HOUSEHOLD TACKS

DOUBLE POINTED TACK

UPHOLS-TERER'S TACK

WIRE UPHOLS-TERER'S TACK

BILL POSTER TACK

GIMP TACK

CHECKER HEAD CARPET TACK

COMMON NAILS		
SIZE	LENGTH	APPROX. NO. PER POUND
2d	1"	845
3d	1¼"	540
4d	1½"	290
5d	1¾"	250
6d	2"	165
7d	2¼"	150
8d	2½"	100
9d	2¾"	90
10d	3"	65
12d	3¼"	60
16d	3½"	45
20d	4"	30

FINISHING NAILS		
3d	1¼"	880
4d	1½"	630
6d	2"	290
8d	2½"	195
10d	3"	125

CASING NAILS		
4d	1½"	490
6d	2"	245
8d	2½"	145
10d	3"	95
16d	3½"	72

HANDY REFERENCE-SCREWS

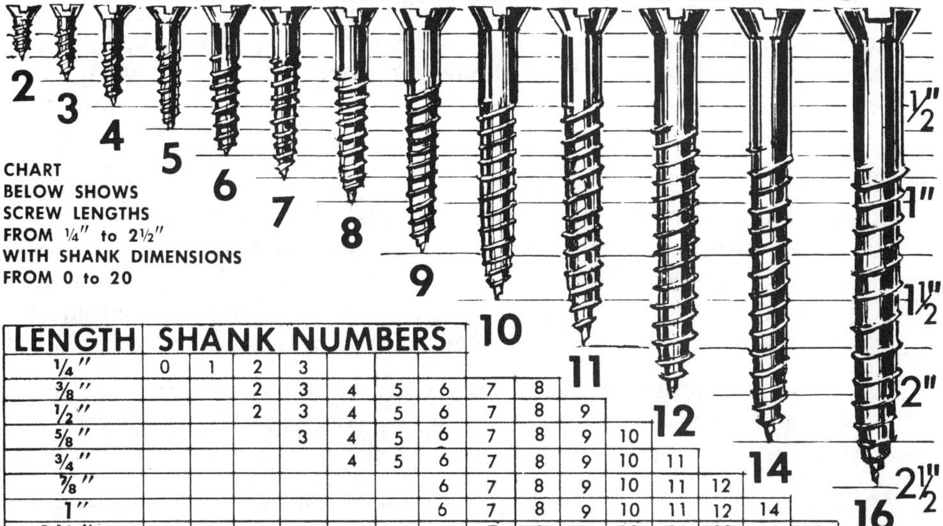

2
3
4
5
6
7
8
9
10
11
12
14
16
1/2"
1"
1 1/2"
2"
2 1/2"

CHART BELOW SHOWS SCREW LENGTHS FROM 1/4" to 2 1/2" WITH SHANK DIMENSIONS FROM 0 to 20

LENGTH	SHANK NUMBERS																
1/4"	0	1	2	3													
3/8"			2	3	4	5	6	7	8								
1/2"			2	3	4	5	6	7	8	9							
5/8"				3	4	5	6	7	8	9	10						
3/4"					4	5	6	7	8	9	10	11					
7/8"							6	7	8	9	10	11	12				
1"							6	7	8	9	10	11	12	14			
1 1/4"								7	8	9	10	11	12	14	16		
1 1/2"							6	7	8	9	10	11	12	14	16	18	
1 3/4"									8	9	10	11	12	14	16	18	20
2"									8	9	10	11	12	14	16	18	20
2 1/4"										9	10	11	12	14	16	18	20

TWIST BIT SIZES for Round, Flat and Oval Head Screws in Drilling Shank and Pilot Holes.

SHANK HOLE Hard & Soft Wood	1/16	5/64	3/32	7/64	7/64	1/2	9/64	5/32	11/64	3/16	3/16	13/64	7/32	1/4	17/64	19/64	21/64
PILOT HOLE Soft Wood	1/64	1/32	1/32	3/64	3/64	1/16	1/16	1/16	5/64	5/64	3/32	3/32	7/64	7/64	9/64	9/64	11/64
PILOT HOLE Hard Wood	1/32	1/32	3/64	1/16	1/16	5/64	5/64	3/32	3/32	7/64	7/64	1/8	1/8	9/64	5/32	3/16	13/64
AUGER BIT sizes for countersunk heads			3	4	4	4	5	5	6	6	6	7	7	8	9	10	11

HOW TO MEASURE

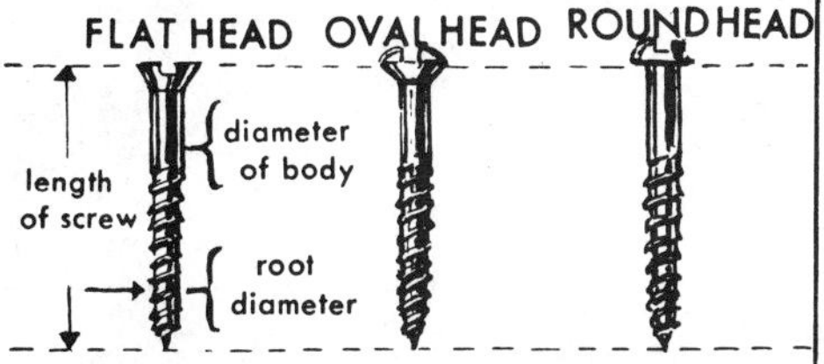

FLAT HEAD
OVAL HEAD
ROUND HEAD
diameter of body
length of screw
root diameter

SHEET METAL SCREWS

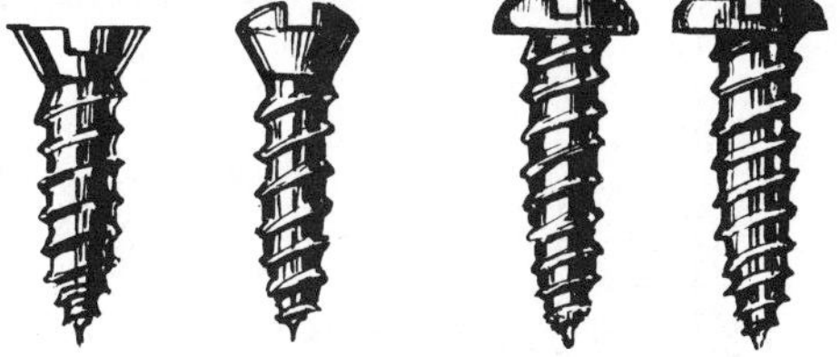

FLAT HEAD
OVAL HEAD
ROUND HEAD
BINDING HEAD

PILOT HOLE

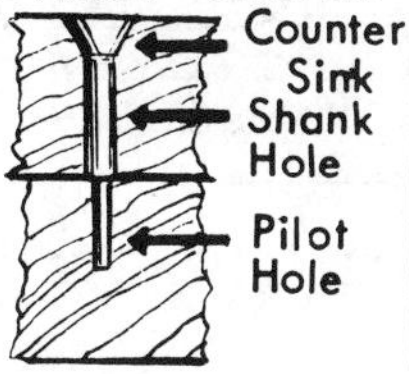

Counter Sink
Shank Hole
Pilot Hole

PHILLIPS SCREW

COUNTER SUNK WASHER

FLUSH TYPE WASHER

FLAT WASHER

HOW TO THINK METRIC

Government officials concerned with the adoption of the metric system are quick to warn anyone from attempting to make precise conversions. One quickly accepts this advice when they begin to convert yards to meters or vice versa. Place a metric ruler alongside a foot ruler and you get the message fast.

Since a meter equals 1.09361 yards, or 39⅜"+, the decimals can drive you up a creek. The government men suggest accepting a rough, rather than exact equivalent. They recommend considering a meter in the same way you presently use a yard. A kilometer as 0.6 of a mile. A kilogram or kilo as just over two pounds. A liter, a quart, with a small extra swig.

To more fully appreciate why a rough conversion is preferable, note the 6" rule alongside the metric rule. A meter contains 100 centimeters. A centimeter contains 10 millimeters.

As an introduction to the metric system, we used a metric rule to measure standard U.S. building materials. Since a 1 x 2 measures anywhere from ¾ to 25/32 x 1½", which is typical of U.S. lumber sizes, the metric equivalents shown are only approximate.

Consider 1" equal to 2.54 centimeters; 10" = 25.4cm.

To multiply 4¼" into centimeters: $4.25 \times 2.54 = 10.795$ or 10.8cm.

INCH	—	MILLIMETER
1"		25.4
15/16		23.8
7/8		22.2
13/16		20.6
3/4		19.0
11/16		17.5
5/8		15.9
9/16		14.3
1/2		12.7
7/16		11.1
3/8		9.5
5/16		7.9
1/4		6.4
3/16		4.8
1/8		3.2
1/16		1.6

INCHES		—	CENTIMETERS
1			2.54
	1/8		2.9
		1/4	3.2
	3/8		3.5
		1/2	3.8
	5/8		4.1
		3/4	4.4
	7/8		4.8
2			5.1
	1/8		5.4
		1/4	5.7
	3/8		6.0
		1/2	6.4
	5/8		6.7
		3/4	7.0
	7/8		7.3
3			7.6
	1/8		7.9
		1/4	8.3
	3/8		8.6
		1/2	8.9
	5/8		9.2
		3/4	9.5
	7/8		9.8

Inches	cm		Inches	cm
4	10.2		11	27.9
1/8	10.5		1/8	28.3
1/4	10.8		1/4	28.6
3/8	11.1		3/8	28.9
1/2	11.4		1/2	29.2
5/8	11.7		5/8	29.5
3/4	12.1		3/4	29.8
7/8	12.4		7/8	30.2
5	12.7		12	30.5
1/8	13.0		1/8	30.8
1/4	13.3		1/4	31.1
3/8	13.7		3/8	31.4
1/2	14.0		1/2	31.8
5/8	14.3		5/8	32.1
3/4	14.6		3/4	32.4
7/8	14.9		7/8	32.7
6	15.2		14	35.6
1/8	15.6		16	40.6
1/4	15.9		20	50.8
3/8	16.2		30	76.2
1/2	16.5		40	101.6
5/8	16.8		50	127.0
3/4	17.1		60	152.4
7/8	17.5		70	177.8
7	17.8		80	203.2
1/8	18.1		90	228.6
1/4	18.4		100	254.0
3/8	18.7			
1/2	19.1			
5/8	19.4			
3/4	19.7			
7/8	20.0			
8	20.3			
1/8	20.6			
1/4	21.0			
3/8	21.3			
1/2	21.6			
5/8	21.9			
3/4	22.2			
7/8	22.5			
9	22.9			
1/8	23.2			
1/4	23.5			
3/8	23.8			
1/2	24.1			
5/8	24.4			
3/4	24.8			
7/8	25.1			
10	25.4			
1/8	25.7			
1/4	26.0			
3/8	26.4			
1/2	26.7			
5/8	27.0			
3/4	27.3			
7/8	27.6			

FEET = INCHES = CENTIMETERS

FEET		INCHES		CENTIMETERS
1 =		12	=	30.5
2 =		24	=	61.0
3 =		36	=	91.4
4 =		48	=	121.9
5 =		60	=	152.4
6 =		72	=	182.9
7 =		84	=	213.4
8 =		96	=	243.8
9 =		108	=	274.3
10 =		120	=	304.8
11 =		132	=	335.3
12 =		144	=	365.8
13 =		156	=	396.2
14 =		168	=	426.7
15 =		180	=	457.2
16 =		192	=	487.7
17 =		204	=	518.2
18 =		216	=	548.6
19 =		228	=	579.1
20 =		240	=	609.6

INDEX TO MONEY SAVING REPAIRS, IMPROVEMENTS, PATTERNS AND BOOKS
(Number designates Easi-Bild Pattern or Book)

144

147

EASI-BILD LEARN TO EARN BOOKS

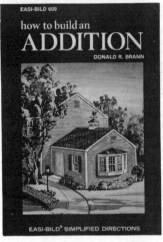

#850 HOW TO FIND A JOB, START A BUSINESS

Of special interest to teens, retirees and anyone who wants to earn extra income. Learn to offer what others want to buy. No capital investment required. 210 pp., 304 illus.

#609 HOW TO BUILD AN ADDITION

Creating additional living space can prove to be one of today's soundest investments. Step-by-step directions explain how to build a 12 x 16', 16 x 24' or any other size one or two story addition, with or without an outside entry. 162pp., 211 illus., simplify every step.

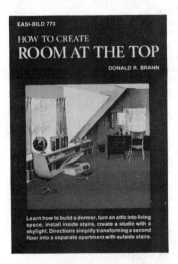

#615 HOW TO MODERNIZE A BASEMENT

Whether you create a family room or turn a basement into an income producing one bedroom apartment with an outside entrance, you will find all the information needed. It explains how to install an outside entry, build stairs, frame partitions, panel walls, lay floor tile and much more. 98pp., 135 illus.

#773 HOW TO CREATE ROOM AT THE TOP

Transform an attic into extra bedrooms or an income producing apartment. Learn how to build a dormer, install a skylight, build inside and outside stairs. Creating living space provides a key to financial survival. This book tells ALL. 162pp. 239 illus.

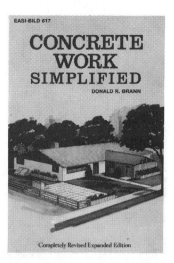

#617 CONCRETE WORK SIMPLIFIED

This book explains everything you need to know to mix concrete, floating, finishing, grooving, edging and pointing, to setting ironwork and anchor bolts. It also explains how to waterproof a basement, install a sump pump, an outside entry and make all kinds of concrete repairs. 194pp., 257 illus.

#668 BRICKLAYING SIMPLIFIED

All who seek income, peace of mind, an economical solution to a costly problem or employment in a trade where opportunity is unlimited, find this book a real guide to better living. It explains how to lay bricks, a wall, walk, veneer a house, build a barbecue, etc. It turns amateurs into pros. 146pp., 212 illus.

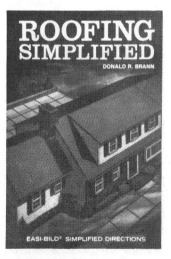

#896 ROOFING SIMPLIFIED

This business of your own book turns amateurs into professional roofers. Learn to apply or replace asphalt, fiberglass, wood, slate, tile and/or roll roofing. Make needed repairs, a roofer's safety harness, work on a roof with no fear of falling. 176pp., 243 illus.

#697 FORMS, FOOTINGS, FOUNDATIONS, FRAMING, STAIR BUILDING

This book tells every reader how to get into the building industry. Whether you build your own house, buy a prefab or want a career in building, this book tells everything you need to know about forms, footings, foundations, framing and stair building. 210pp., 310 illus.

#758 HOW TO MODERNIZE A KITCHEN
Of special interest to homeowners who appreciate the convenience and Capital Gains of a completely modernized kitchen. Directions explain how to build base and wall cabinets to fit any space available or modernize existing wood or metal cabinets. Plan the kitchen that fills your family needs today and in the future. 210pp., 263 illus.

#674 HOW TO INSTALL A FIREPLACE
Everyone who wants to install a woodburning stove, build a brick fireplace or install a prefabricated metal fireplace and chimney, will find all the direction they need. Installing a chimney completely within or recessed flush with an outside wall is clearly explained and illustrated. 242pp., 354 illus.

#683 CARPETING SIMPLIFIED
Laying carpet in your home can provide the experience needed to do the same work for others. Step-by-step directions explain how to install every type of carpeting over any kind of floor, with or without padding. Learn how to carpet stairs, install under-carpet electronic alarm mats and more. 178pp., 223 illus.

**#695 HOW TO INSTALL
PROTECTIVE ALARM DEVICES**
Recapture peace of mind by protecting all doors and windows with professional devices. Discourage a break-in with magnetic contacts that automatically notify policy, install alarm bells, detect movement instantly with easy to install radar. A layman's guide to professional installation of alarm devices. 130pp.,146 illus.

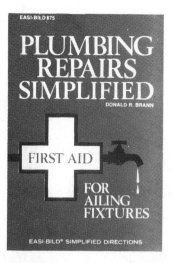

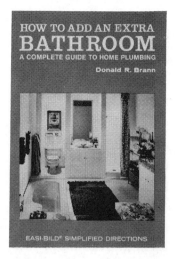

#875 PLUMBING REPAIRS SIMPLIFIED

Homeowners who dislike having their budget and peace of mind destroyed by a costly plumbing repair find this book helps save time, temper and money. Read, learn, then do what directions suggest and see how easily you can replace parts and make repairs like a pro. 226pp., 841 illus.

#682 HOW TO ADD AN EXTRA BATHROOM

This complete, easy to read guide to home plumbing helps make a dream come true for only the cost of fixtures. Directions explain how to make the installation and save a bundle. Those who don't want to do any plumbing still save by preparing the area, then having a plumber make the installation. 162pp., 200 illus.

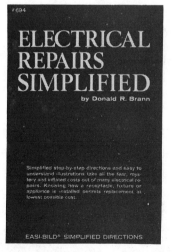

#694 ELECTRICAL REPAIRS SIMPLIFIED

Learning to economically make electrical repairs not only generates peace of mind, but also income in your spare time. This book takes the fear, mystery and inflated cost out of many troublesome repairs. A special feature explains how to install wiring in a dollhouse. 134pp., 218 illus.

#816 HOW TO LAY CERAMIC TILE

Learn how to apply ceramic and quarry tile to floor, walls, countertops and patios. Information about tools, materials, surface preparation, special situations and valuable time saving trade tips included. Directions explain how to build a quarry tile pad for woodburning stoves, how to apply decorative tile around a fireplace and more. 178pp., 225 illus.

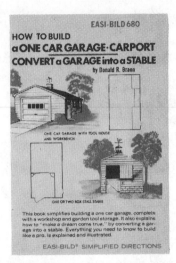

#663 HOW TO BUILD A TWO CAR GARAGE, LEAN-TO PORCH, CABANA

Building a garage can prove to be a richly rewarding experience. Letters from readers who built this garage confirm the task altered their outlook on life. Many who build turn it into an income producing singles apartment. 130pp., 142 illus.

#680 HOW TO BUILD A ONE CAR GARAGE, CARPORT, CONVERT A GARAGE INTO A STABLE

Building a one car garage with ample space for a workshop, or turning a one car garage into a two box stall stable is clearly explained. Directions tell how to raise a garage to obtain needed headroom, build a carport, lean-to toolhouse and a cupola. 146pp., 181 illus.

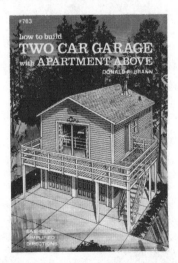

#684 HOW TO TRANSFORM A GARAGE INTO LIVING SPACE

Transforming a garage into a living-bedroom, with a kitchen and bathroom, can provide a safe and economical solution to a costly nursing home problem. It can also become an important income producer. Step-by-step directions explain every step. 130pp., 139 illus.

#763 HOW TO BUILD A TWO CAR GARAGE WITH APARTMENT ABOVE

Build a two car, two story garage or add a second story apartment to an existing garage. Space above provides a living, bedroom, kitchen and bathroom. Ideal for a single or couple. 194pp., 226 illus.

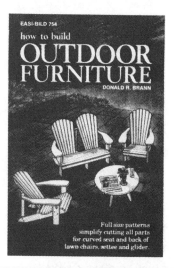

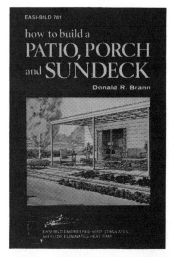

#754 HOW TO BUILD OUTDOOR FURNITURE
Easy to follow step-by-step directions, plus a big foldout full size pattern, simplify tracing and cutting all parts to exact shape required. Learn how to build curved back lawn chairs, a matching settee, four passenger lawn glider, a chaise on wheels and much, much more. 162pp., 176 illus., plus full size pattern.

#781 HOW TO BUILD A PATIO, PORCH AND SUNDECK
Simplified directions take all the inflated cost out of building a front or back porch, a patio to length and width specified or to size desired, a carport and sundeck. Every step, from laying footings to installation of railings, is illustrated. Make screens, porch repairs, swimming pool enclosure and much more. 146pp., 220 illus.

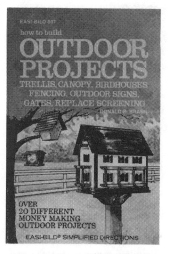

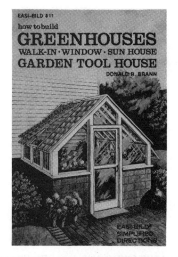

#807 HOW TO BUILD OUTDOOR PROJECTS
Directions explain how to make over 20 outdoor projects. Learn to repair and replace window and door screening, build gates and fencing, door canopy, trellis, outdoor planter, signs, birdhouses, feeders and more. 210 pp., 212 illus.

#811 HOW TO BUILD GREENHOUSES — WALK-IN, WINDOW, SUNHOUSE, GARDEN TOOL HOUSE
Of special interest to everyone who enjoys the fun and relaxation of growing plants the year round. The sunhouse appeals to sun lovers who enjoy winter sunbathing. 210pp., 229 illus.

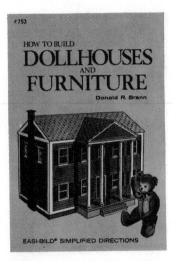

#753 HOW TO BUILD DOLLHOUSES & FURNITURE
To create a memory a little girl will never forget, build one of the three dollhouses offered in this book. Those searching for a part or full time money making hobby find a ready market for dollhouses. Full size patterns simplify making fourteen pieces of dollhouse furniture. 194pp., 316 illus.

#757 HOW TO BUILD A KAYAK
Simplified directions and full size frame patterns permit building this extremely light yet sturdy kayak to three different lengths, 14'3", 16'9", or 18'0". It can easily be carried on a cartop rack and used by one or two adults. Patterns insure cutting each frame to exact size required. This book includes full size patterns for all frames.

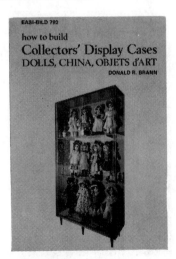

#771 TOYMAKING AND CHILDREN'S FURNITURE SIMPLIFIED
As every reader soon discovers, toymaking possesses a certain magic. Directions for pony ride rocker, giraffe clothes tree, bunk beds, toy chest and 12 other projects included. 226pp., 330 illus., plus a full size foldout pattern.

#792 HOW TO BUILD COLLECTORS' DISPLAY CASES
Learn to build handsome, clear acrylic, museum quality, floor, table top and wall display cabinets. These provide the perfect way to display every kind of possession from dolls, china, figurines, etc. Retailers buy these cases for store use as readily as for resale. 194pp., 229 illus.

#756 SCROLL SAW PROJECTS

Helping everyone, a child or retiree, success-fully turn a piece of wood into a handsome, useable and saleable article, builds the ego. This book insures success. 27 full size patterns permit tracing all parts, then assembling each in exact position shown on pattern. 130pp., 146 illus.

#669 HOW TO BUILD BIRDHOUSES AND BIRD FEEDERS

Encouraging a child to build feeders and bird-houses can stimulate a lifetime interest in woodworking. Full size patterns not only simplify building but also insure success. Helping a child turn a piece of wood into a useable and saleable article builds instant self confidence. 66pp., 86 illus.

#679 HOW TO BUILD A STABLE AND RED BARN TOOL HOUSE

A 20x30' three box stall stable is easy to build. Every step of construction, from selecting a site to building the cupola, is explained and illustrated. Directions also simplify building an 8x10' or larger tool house. 178pp., 197 illus.

#751 HOW TO BUILD PET HOUSING

Encourage all who love pets to build the shelter each needs. Learn how to build a doghouse, lean-to kennel, rabbit hutch, duck-inn, parakeet cage, an all weather cat entry, plus a unique catpartment that's easy to sell, easy to rent. 178pp., 252 illus.

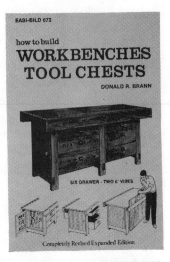

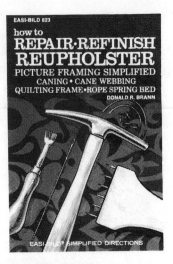

#672 HOW TO BUILD WORKBENCHES
Every home, apartment and place of business needs a workbench to economically make repairs and improvements. Build a 6' workbench with a 6' vise on one or both sides, big drawers and tool compartments. Directions for foldaway wall benches that require only a minimum of floor space also included. 180pp., 250 illus., plus full size foldout pattern.

#823 HOW TO REPAIR, REFINISH, REUPHOLSTER
Learn to apply first aid to ailing furniture. Reglue joints, replace tenons, torn webbing, springs, etc. Make a 28" picture frame clamp, a professional mat cutting board, a rope spring bed, and a 114" quilting frame. Everything you need to kow from tacks to tools. 176pp., 215illus.

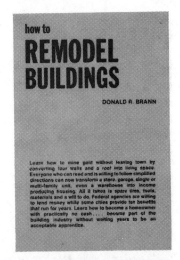

#605 HOW TO INSTALL PANELING
Learn to apply paneling like a pro. Building a matching wall to wall storage closet with sliding doors, a fireplace mantel, install valances with indirect lighting, even build a cedar lined storage room. 146pp., 214 illus., plus full size valance patterns simplify every step.

#685 HOW TO REMODEL BUILDINGS
With abandoned big city housing units available to all who are willing to rehabilitate and occupy same, this book explains how to become a landlord with an investment of time and effort. It tells how to turn an abandoned multi-family building, store, garage or warehouse into rentable housing. Every step explained and illustrated. 258pp.,345 illus.

160

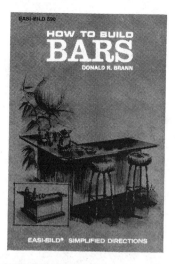

#690 HOW TO BUILD BARS
Building a bar offers a fun way to furnish a recreation room. Learning to build a straight, L-shaped or any of the seven bars described provides an easy way to start a part or full time business. Doing something today you didn't know how to do yesterday broadens one's sphere of activity. 162pp., 195 illus.

#804 HOW TO BUILD BOOKCASES
AND STEREO CABINETS
Takes all the mystery and ⅔ the cost out of building bookcases and cabinets to fill any space available. Directions explain how to build wall-to-wall, built-in, free standing and sectional bookcases and stereo cabinets. 194pp., 232 illus.

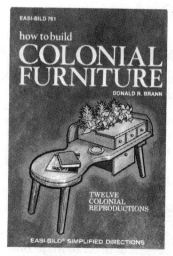

#630 HOW TO BUILD SPORTSMAN'S
REVOLVING STORAGE CABINET
Directions simplify building a glass enclosed gun cabinet, wall racks and a 24 x 72" revolving cabinet that stores everything from guns to clothing. Learn to make what others want to buy. 98pp., 121 illus.

#761 HOW TO BUILD COLONIAL FURNITURE
You can easily obtain furniture at a fraction of retail cost by building colonial reproductions. Easy to follow directions and full size patterns simplify building a cobbler's bench, hutch cabinet, blanket chest, under the eaves rope bed, wall cabinet and more. 258pp., 342 illus.

161

EASI-BILD 832

how to build a
LOW COST HOUSE
ABOVE or BELOW GROUND
DONALD R. BRANN

EASI-BILD® SIMPLIFIED DIRECTIONS

how to
FIND A JOB
START A BUSINESS
Learn to Offer what Others want to Buy
No Capital Investment Required

3 BEDROOM
FOUNDATION
HOUSE

ISBN 0-87733-832-9 ● METRIC CONVERSION SCALE INCLUDED ● PRINTED IN U.S.A.

#832 HOW TO BUILD A LOW COST HOUSE – ABOVE OR BELOW GROUND
A one story house over a full basement with cross ventilation, can provide low cost, energy saving shelter. With one bedroom on the first floor, and either one or two in the basement, it offers an amazing amount of living space. Those who prefer builing an extended foundation, embanked by earth on three sides, discover its even less costly to heat in winter, cool in summer. Step by step directions take all the fear, mystery and inflated costs out of building a three-bedroom house. 226pp. 177 illus.

LIMITED EDITIONS STILL AVAILABLE

#603 How to Build a Dormer—82pp.,114 illus.

#606 How to Lay Ceramic Tile—98pp.,137 illus.

#607 How to Build Fences,Gates,Outdoor Projects—162pp.,212 illus.

#608 How to Modernize a Kitchen—82pp.,118 illus.

#611 How to Build Greenhouses—114pp.,110 illus.

**#612 How to Build Wall-to-Wall Cabinets,
Stereo Installation Simplified**—130pp.,165 illus.

#613 How to Build or Enclose a Porch—82pp.,112 illus.

#623 How to Repair,Refinish and Reupholster Furniture — 98pp.,138illus.

**#627 How to Make Cornice Boards, Draperies,
Valances, Install Traverse Track**—66pp.,117 illus.

#631 How to Build Patios and Sundecks—98pp.,133 illus.

#634 How to Build Storage Units—98pp.,145 illus.

#649 How to Build a Garden Toolhouse,Child's Playhouse—82pp.,107 illus.

**#658 How to Build Kitchen Cabinets,
Room Dividers and Cabinet Furniture**—98pp.,134 illus.

#664 How to Construct Built-In and Sectional Bookcases—98pp.,137 illus.

#665 How to Modernize an Attic—82pp.,86 illus.

#677 How to Plan and Build a Home Workshop—98pp.,133 illus.

#696 Roofing Simplified—130 pp., 168 illus.